Distant Strangers

BERKELEY SERIES IN BRITISH STUDIES

Edited by Mark Bevir and James Vernon

Distant Strangers

How Britain Became Modern

James Vernon

UNIVERSITY OF CALIFORNIA PRESS

Berkeley Los Angeles London

University of California Press, one of the most
distinguished university presses in the United States,
enriches lives around the world by advancing scholarship
in the humanities, social sciences, and natural sciences. Its
activities are supported by the UC Press Foundation and
by philanthropic contributions from individuals and
institutions. For more information, visit www.ucpress.edu.

University of California Press
Berkeley and Los Angeles, California

University of California Press, Ltd.
London, England

Berkeley Series in British Studies, Vol. 9

Library of Congress Cataloging-in-Publication Data

Vernon, James, 1965—
    Distant strangers : how Britain became modern / James
Vernon.
        pages cm.—(Berkeley series in British studies, vol. 9)
    Includes bibliographical references and index.
    ISBN 978-0-520-28203-2 (cloth : alk. paper) —
    ISBN 978-0-520-28204-9 (pbk. : alk. paper) —
    ISBN 978-0-520-95778-7 (e-book)
    1. Great Britain—Civilization.   2. Social change—
Great Britain—History.   3. Civilization, Modern.
4. Civilization, Modern—British influences.   I. Title.
    DA110.V47 2014
    941—dc23
                                            2013045356

Manufactured in the United States of America

23 22 21 20 19 18 17 16 15 14
10 9 8 7 6 5 4 3 2 1

To Alf

CONTENTS

LIST OF FIGURES

PREFACE

This book explores the greatest historical transformation of the past three centuries and quite possibly of all time. It asks how we became modern and examines the character of modern life that is sometimes described as "modernity." It does so by showing how a profoundly new and modern social condition emerged in Britain between the middle of the eighteenth and the end of the nineteenth centuries. The rapid expansion of the population, and its increasing mobility over ever-greater distances, created a society of strangers. This raised a series of problems for the conduct of economic, political, and social life. Old forms of authority, association, and exchange, rooted in personal and local relations, were increasingly inadequate or impossible. They were slowly displaced by increasingly abstract and bureaucratic ways of making economic, social, and political relations between distant strangers possible. Yet this did not lead to the disenchantment of the modern world, because new forms of bureaucratic abstraction catalyzed, and were made possible by, a reanimation of the local and the personal. The modern condition was, then, not just the novel experience of living in a society of strangers but the dialectical process through which the forms of authority, affect, and exchange were remade.

There are good reasons to suggest that Britain was the first country to undergo this transformation and become modern. I am, however, less interested in whether Britain was the first modern society or made the modern world (as countless book titles and university classes have suggested) than in whether this understanding of modernity makes sense when applied elsewhere. In the past few decades, historians, like other social scientists, have come to believe that every society can become modern in its own way and that there are a potentially infinite number of alternative experiences of modernity. It is my contention that this evacuates the term modernity of any meaning or analytical utility. So the real purpose of this book, and the reason why it might be of interest to people not interested in Britain, is to suggest that if the category of modernity is to be at all analytically useful it must capture a singular condition or process that all societies experience, albeit in their own peculiar ways.

So unfashionable is this argument that I need to begin by explaining why I am making it. Over the past generation historians have contrived to make history more interesting by emphasizing how less and less happened. For sure, we have made history more democratic by making it global and including more and more people, animals, and even things, but our explanations of historical change have become so complex that we are in danger of making history decidedly uneventful. Nowhere is this more apparent than in the history of Europe. From the late nineteenth century, the modern discipline of history arose to make sense of Europe's past, and it did so around a clear narrative of the making of the modern world (sometimes described in the United States as the rise of Western civilization). That story was punctuated by a series of foundational and transformative events like the Renaissance, the Reformation, the Enlightenment, the Industrial Revolution, and the rise of the nation-state. As historians have become more suspicious of this narrative, more conscious of those people in Europe excluded from it and of the rival claims of other historical civilizations, they have revised and qualified it. All those once foundational events are now considered to have a more complex history. They are portrayed as less transformative, the result of long and uneven processes of change that spread over centuries and increasingly generous geographies. The old history of one damned revolutionary transformation after another has given way to a more modest history of continuities and uncertainties.

As Britain often held a fabled place in the latter stages of this history as the home of the Industrial Revolution, it became an important historiographical battleground. The first signs of the gathering storm were evident in the 1930s when Sellar and Yeatman's *1066 and All That* parodied the triumphalist "drums and trumpet" version of British history taught in schools, and J. H. Clapham's voluminous *An Economic History of Modern Britain* queried the rapidity and scale of Britain's Industrial Revolution. The clouds burst after the Second World War, when American modernization theory celebrated what it portrayed as Britain's almost miraculous combination of rapid industrialization with relative political and social stability. By the 1970s, few historians accepted such a view and emphasized instead the scale of social and political conflict in the face of the stubborn grip of Britain's *ancien regime* and the *long duree* of its economic transformation. Big-bang models of change gave way to ones characterized by long and uneven whimpers. For some, Britain had not only not made the modern world but had never been modern herself.

There was, of course, a politics to all this. During the 1960s and 1970s, the trope of "decline" was variously used to understand Britain's loss of its empire, the repositioning of its economy in an increasingly competitive global environment, the apparent breakup of the nation-state with the rise of Irish, Scottish, and Welsh nationalism, the rise of multiculturalism in an increasingly racially and religious diverse country, and the seeming collapse of moral and industrial order. Politicians on the right, not least those associated with the rise of what became known as Thatcherism, saw revisionist academic histories that played down Britain's part in the making of the modern world as part of a culture of declinism that had to be arrested if the country was to be made Great again. This debate, between supposedly leftist revisionist historians and those on the right looking to restore Britain and her history to their former glories, was played out in 1988 during Margaret Thatcher's second term of government with the development of a new national curriculum for the teaching of history in schools. It has recently reignited as a new Conservative-led government has once again promised to redress the way that children leave school apparently ignorant of what Minister of Education Michael Gove described as "one of the most inspiring stories I know—the history of our United Kingdom." Desiring the return of a narrative history of the nation (albeit without so many drums and trumpets), and believing that those who teach history in schools and universities have lost the plot, he recruited populist TV dons to develop a new curriculum that historians have greeted with almost universal opprobrium.

Across the Atlantic, the fear of the decline of British history has manifested itself differently. In 1998 the North American Conference on British Studies commissioned some of its leading historians of Britain to assess the state of their field. Published the following year, the so-called Stansky Report was a depressing document. Long on anecdote and short on data, it lamented the marginalization of British history at all levels—the dwindling interest of undergraduates, the lack of funding and jobs for graduate students, and the diminishing opportunities to publish in the mainstream academic journals and presses. In this reading, British history was the victim of the culture wars in the American and Canadian academies, which had branded British history as that of DWM (Dead White Men) and encouraged history departments to replace historians of Britain with those of other parts of the world. The report's prescription for this malaise was for British historians to take an imperial turn that acknowledged the contagious and exploitive presence of empire. This is now the orthodoxy of the field in the United States, where the history of imperial Britain has new resonance as America has increasingly trodden in the shadows of the British Empire by intervening in the very regions once colonized by Britain. All of a sudden, whether one is a champion or critic (and *there are* champions who have suggested that America can learn from Britain's imperial example!), the story of the rise and fall of the world's first modern imperial superpower looks uncannily relevant.

For the most part, historians of Britain have felt blind sided by the calls to restore a triumphalist national narrative and recognize the positive contribution of the British Empire in making the modern world. The past two generations of professional scholarship have arguably not equipped us well to counter such egregious claims. The rise of social and cultural history from the 1970s placed new emphases on the thick descriptions of microhistories and made many historians (myself included) allergic to the grand explanatory ambitions and macroaccounts of historical change that so bewitched an earlier generation. It is probably not a coincidence that this occurred as the discipline became increasingly fragmented in to ever-more specialist subdisciplines (structured by subject, chronology, and method) and the restructuring of universities transformed the nature of academic labor by insisting we publish more despite the proliferation of administrative duties and the growing number of students to teach. As we historians have said more and more about less and less, university administrations and politicians alike have questioned the value of our discipline. In Britain, public funding for the teaching of history at universities, like those of other subjects in the arts, humanities, and social sciences, has been entirely removed, and some history departments have closed.

So for me, returning to a big historical question like the transition to modernity seems a timely way of demonstrating how the work of history still matters and has public value. Regaining our confidence to develop macroexplanations of historical change may allow the public to make better sense of the past and our present. I am not alone in this endeavor, and there are different ways of doing it. The relatively new fields of "Big" and "World" or "Global" history have dramatically expanded the chronological and geographical range and explanatory scale of the discipline. Yet they have done so by raising troubling intellectual and institutional questions about the extent to which they obscure the specificity of particular national histories, the capacity to teach them, and the ability to do research in their own languages. Why hire a historian of China, India, Brazil, or Russia, let alone an ancient, medieval, early modern or modern historian when a World or Big historian would do? Indeed, for Bill Gates, a prominent supporter of Big History and the move to remote online models of education, one imagines a single MOOC (Massive Open Online Class) on History would suffice!

In this context my endeavor seems modest indeed. For in seeking to explain how Britain became modern I am returning to the perennial problem that has haunted historians, namely, how the modern world is different from those that had previously existed in the ancient, medieval, and early modern periods. History as a discipline is organized around these epochs, and if we cannot explain how modernity is different, how we got there, and in what ways people across the world share a common experience of it, then we should not be surprised that politicians, university administrators, students, and the public at large lose interest in what we do.

Trying to make sense of modernity in the way I do here certainly involves compromises and risks. Big questions not only invite debate, but they invariably require authors to trespass onto less familiar territory. This is decidedly not a research monograph; it is written more in the style of a long essay or a series of lectures. There will be some who will be unimpressed by an interpretive work of synthesis that draws heavily on the research of others, albeit in ways they might not have anticipated. While I have tried to be diligent about acknowledging when I am using or referring to the work of others, I have also kept the scholarly apparatus of countless footnotes to a minimum. My hope is that while this approach will disappoint those enduring exams or looking for mountains of new research, it will make the book both easier and more interesting to read.

Last, there are the usual and very necessary thanks to all those who have helped make the writing of this book possible. I am enormously lucky to have spent twenty years working with incredibly gifted graduate students. Many of them will see in these pages traces of their own work and of conversations within and beyond the classroom. A Mellon-funded program that allowed faculty and students at Berkeley, Chicago, Yale, and Texas to debate the nature and timing of Britain's transition to modernity was enormously stimulating, not least because of the energy and arguments of my coorganizer Steve Pincus. Penny Ismay is in some respects a coauthor so long have we worried about what a history of modernity might look like. Trevor Jackson not only helped me get the demographic numbers right but got me over the finishing line. My thanks to all those who endured reading papers or earlier drafts and helped me figure out what I was saying and how to say it better: David Anixter, Mary Elizabeth Berry, Venus Bivar, Paul Duguid, Desmond FitzGibbon, Grahame Foreman, John Gillis, Penny Ismay, Patrick Joyce, Seth Koven, Thomas Laqueur, Jon Lawrence, Thomas Metcalf, Chris Otter, Peter Sahlins, Tehila Sasson, Priya Satia, Yuri Slezkine, Randy Starn, Jan de Vries, David Vincent, Daniel Ussishkin, and Wen-hsin Yeh. I am also grateful to those at the Social History Society conference in Manchester 2011, the Vanderbilt History Seminar in Spring 2012, and Berkeley's History Department Colloquium in Spring 2013 for their comments and questions. Conrad Leyser and Matt Houlbrook organized a lecture and workshop in Oxford in Fall 2012 that was both fun and fruitful. Niels Hooper restored my faith in academic publishing and stepped in where others feared to tread; Kim Hogeland and Francisco Reinking shepherded me through the press; Pam Suwinsky gamely tried to redeem my subliterate prose; Nick Kardahji compiled the index.

This book has been written in turbulent times. While financiers led the world to ruins, my own family has been dealing with its own crises and all those dear to me have had to cling to each other as though our lives depended on it. Through all of this my sisters Clare and Binni have been pillars of strength and support. So too have their husbands and their hordes of (now adult!) children—as well as, of course, my mother Stella. Nothing is imaginable or bearable without Ros and our children Jack, Mischa, and Alf. It is them and their love that keeps me going. This one is for you, Alf. I am so glad you are with us (better to arrive late than never) even if you do insist on supporting the wrong team.

CHAPTER ONE

What Is Modernity?

Wherever they live and in whatever condition, most people across the world consider themselves modern, even though they have very different understandings of what that means. It is easier to say what modernity is not than what it is. It is not a place or territory; you don't know you have arrived by a stamp in your passport. It is not a date or moment that when it arrives transports you into the modern world. It is neither an attitude nor the product of a modernist aesthetic. So what is modernity? How do we know who is modern and when they became so?

These questions have preoccupied many of the finest social scientists over the past two centuries. Despite the many differences in their accounts, most accept that becoming modern is a process that entails the demolition of "traditional" forms of life and the construction of new, "modern" alternatives to them. In the late nineteenth and early twentieth centuries, the founding fathers of the social sciences viewed this process as revolutionary and endowed it with an inexorable logic that would eventually transform the entire world. They advanced two competing types of analysis: one emphasizing economic and social conditions; the other cultural, political, and institutional ones. They were not by any means mutually exclusive forms of explanation. Most accepted that all these domains of life were dramatically transformed;

rather the argument was over where causal responsibility lay—was it economic changes that led to cultural ones or vice versa, did social forces generate political changes, and so on. Critically, both sets of explanations were rooted in structural and comparative understandings of change. They sought to explain not just whether the transition to modernity was driven by economic, social, political, or cultural structures but how similar processes of modernization were occurring in different countries at roughly the same time.

Marx never used the term *modernity*, yet he clearly identified the emergence of capitalism in Britain as sweeping away traditional forms of economic and social organization. As he memorably wrote in *The Communist Manifesto,* "Constant revolutionizing of production, uninterrupted disturbance of all social conditions, everlasting uncertainty and agitation distinguish the bourgeois epoch from all earlier ones. All fixed, fast frozen relations, with their train of ancient and venerable prejudices and opinions, are swept away, all new-formed ones become antiquated before they can ossify. All that is solid melts into air, all that is holy is profaned, and man is at last compelled to face with sober senses his real condition of life and his relations with his kind."[1] Many others have followed Marx in considering the creative destruction of industrial capitalism as a central feature of modernity even if they do not always share his analysis of its causes or corrosive effects. Writing almost a century later, Polanyi considered what he called *The Great Transformation* (1944) to be not capitalism and its new forms of production per se but the ideological invention of the free market and the reorganization of social life around it.[2] Polanyi here was writing less against Marx than those who, during the 1940s and 1950s, valorized the free market model of capitalism and used the British case of industrialization as an exemplary world historical model whose stages of economic growth and modernization others should follow.[3]

Just as Marx believed the modern "bourgeois epoch" came with class struggle and the "uninterrupted disturbance of all social conditions," so others have analyzed modernity as the experience of a new set of social conditions. Following Engels's *The Condition of the Working Classes in England* (1844), there has been a good deal of focus on the process of urbanization that was often seen as an effect of workers flooding to jobs in the new urban centers of industrial manufacturing. The recrafting of social relations within these new cities, and their dynamics of antagonism, cohesion, or anomie, preoccupied the classical sociology of Durkheim and Simmel.[4]

These accounts of modernity as an economic or social condition rooted in industrial capitalism and urbanization have not gone unchallenged. Since the late nineteenth century there have been rival accounts that emphasized the cultural, political, and institutional foundations that structure modern life. A key element of these accounts, particularly in their early articulation by Maine, Tonnies, and Weber, was the rise of individualism and its increasing centrality to modern systems of legal, social, and political organization. The polymath Henry Maine—legal theorist, historian, and civil servant—identified the transition from status to contract as the basis of modern civilization. He did so by mapping the ways in which the foundations of legal authority and power changed from systems based on kinship or tribal loyalties to those centered upon the individual and adjudicated by the state. Similarly, the German sociologist Ferdinand Tonnies identified two types of social organization that he termed *Gemeinschaft* and *Gesellschaft*. While the former was characterized by a sense of innate community and the mutuality of social life, the latter denoted an individualism in which voluntary association was instrumental and self-serving. Although he acknowledged that these two social forms could coexist, Tonnies believed that there had been a transition from *Gemeinschaft* to *Geselleschaft* in modern industrial and urban conditions.[5] Finally, Max Weber also placed the rise of the individual at the center of the modern condition. He did so in two ways. First, he found the origins of capitalism in the competitive individualism unleashed by the Protestant Reformation. And, second, he traced the transformation of political authority away from the charismatic forms that ensured specific groups or persons could rule communities to the modern, anonymous bureaucracies that governed subjects through abstract systems of rational control.

Clearly, all these classical accounts of modernity posit a clear separation between the traditional and the modern. One might even say, and many have, that their characterization of the traditional (as archaic, primitive, feudal, etc.—all the terms have pejorative connotations) serves less to accurately describe the past than the distance of the present conditions they seek to analyze and capture.[6] To a certain extent this was the point. The object was to emphasize the historical novelty of systems and conditions that their contemporaries took for granted as natural. Establishing that the way the modern world worked was of relatively recent vintage made it mutable and therefore possible to change again.

And yet these caricatures of the traditional yielded caricatures of the modern. Because the traditional was intended to illuminate the modern, and vice versa, there was no understanding of the forms of imbrication that unsettled any clear distinction between them. Indeed, the transition from the traditional to the modern was portrayed as so absolute and rapid it was frequently described as occurring through a series of revolutions—scientific, agricultural, industrial. These revolutions were invariably seen as sequential, with one unleashing another in a developmental process of what became known as modernization: so that the agricultural revolution made possible industrialization, which catalyzed urbanization. And finally, this process of modernization, although a product of a particular time and place (whether England 1780–1830, or Euro-America 1780–1880), was considered universally relevant. All those who wished to become modern had to follow the prescribed route or remain trapped within the yoke of tradition or prisoners of a bastard modernity. Interest in these classical models of modernization as a dramatically unfolding and universal process waxed during the Cold War as the United States and Soviet Union offered competing models of the modern world.[7]

By the late twentieth century, these theories and accounts of modernization had been discredited. Historians were at the forefront of exposing the fallacies of universal models of historical development that expected, in Edward Thompson's formulation, the working class to "rise like the sun at an appointed time." So too were postcolonial critics who insisted that the modern world did not have to be cast in a Euro-American mold. After all, the West had become modern at the expense of those they enslaved and colonized and then organized supposedly universal laws of historical progress around their own experience.[8] Instead of a trickle-down process of modernization from the West to the Rest, postcolonial critics contended there was no one way to be modern and no checklist of modernization to complete along the way. So compelling were these critiques that by 1995 the term *modernization*, with its portrayal of sequential and unilinear processes of development, had been displaced in academic journals by the seemingly less loaded term *modernity*.[9] Understood in cultural terms as historically specific, there was no longer any one path to becoming modern; instead modernity allowed the modern condition to be pluralized and found in any number of alternative and regional forms across the world.[10] Indeed, as the term *modernity* no longer describes a specific condition or process of transformation, it is often used to describe any context in which the rhetoric of the modern is found. Reduced to a word or vocabulary, the work of analysis is in examining its varied uses and meanings and the politics that lay behind them.[11] In this way modernity has now acquired a whole series of hyphenated prefixes that extend far beyond its regional or national alternatives. Thus a variety of competing conservative, colonial, imperial, suburban, Sapphic, feminine, gendered, and metropolitan modernities have been found in interwar Britain alone![12] For some scholars, modernity now even comes with attitude—it can be dangerous, displaced, refracted. If there is any coherence to this proliferation of modernity's prefixes, it is the attempt to track how different groups assert their interests by laying claim to the language of the modern.

This pluralization of modernity has come at a certain cost. If modernity has become so elastic that it assumes multiple forms and can be found almost everywhere at any historical moment, it is no longer clear whether the term can do any analytical work. Indeed, historians have now discovered a plethora of modern*ities* in all corners of the globe between the sixteenth and twentieth centuries! No wonder we are all confused and some have pleaded that we just do without modernity as a category of analysis and description. Certainly the recent forum on "Historians and the Question of Modernity" in the *American Historical Review* did little to inspire confidence that the term could be rescued.[13] Yet however much historians might want to rid ourselves of this troublesome category, we cannot live without it. We are, after all, in the business of tracing change over time, and we have to move from the particular to the general to do so. Thinking with modernity allows us to mark a moment of historical transition from an earlier period that may have seeded the origins of many aspects of modern life but was nonetheless decidedly different. We need to understand the alterity of the ancient, medieval, and early modern worlds and recognize that they did not always anticipate later developments but represented alternative historical experiences. As a broad and inevitably reductive analytical term *modernity* can also help us explain patterns of historical change that appear to be shared by many countries. Investigating those shared historical processes does not need to reduce them to a universal telos. Rather than returning to a view of modernity as simply emanating from the West to the Rest, the object should be to illuminate not only what is similar or shared but how they are experienced differently in different places and at different times.

Modernization theory was structured around the quest for a single origin or cause that triggered and explained a subsequent path of historical development. Thus capitalism was the product of Europe's Protestant Reformation, which created a new type of individual, organized within monogamous nuclear families, who sought salvation through hard work.[14] Or, more recently, the great divergence of economic fortunes between Europe and China from the eighteenth century has been explained by accidents of geography that placed rich and easily accessed mineral deposits close to industrializing localities.[15] In history, as in life, such golden bullets rarely exist as explanations or solutions, for we inhabit multiple processes of change that converge, clash, and combine, manifesting themselves in sometimes surprising and paradoxical formations. Thus instead of seeking the causal origin of modernization, I use the concept of modernity to capture the nature of the modern condition. I am less interested in *why* societies become modern than in *how* they do so. The aim of this book, then, is to invite the reader to share a particular perspective on what it means to be modern and how we got there.

So how did Britain become modern?[16] I have three answers that structure the argument of this book. Firstly, I aim to show that the sustained growth and increasing mobility of its population, including over an expanding empire, created a new society of strangers. Secondly, I suggest that this generated a range of new challenges for the conduct of social, economic, and political life that had hitherto primarily (if not exclusively) rested upon local and personal relations. Increasingly abstract and bureaucratic forms were used to address the challenges of living around, doing business with, and governing (often distant) strangers. And yet, thirdly, this process of abstraction was dialectical in nature. Just as we have long known that the invention of new traditions was an inseparable part of the experience of modernity, so the new forms of abstraction and estrangement catalyzed attempts to reembed social, economic, and political life in local and personal relations.

It is not my contention that Britons were the first to live or trade with strangers. According to Simmel, the figure of "the stranger" had long played three important roles: they facilitated extra-local trade, provided an objective perspective of those societies they moved through or lived among, and generated more abstract social relations.[17] Although Simmel took his examples from early modern Europe, he might just as well have looked further back to the experience of mass urban life in ancient Rome or further afield to the intercontinental trade networks of the Indian Ocean or the early modern imperial systems of the Ming, the Mughals, and the Ottomans. Yet rather than view the stranger as an exceptional and transhistorical figure, defying the limits of space and time, I suggest that the rapid and *sustained* expansion of populations that were increasingly mobile over greater distances in the modern world created a *society* of strangers. And as Adam Smith suggested, Britons were probably the first to live in a society of strangers. They did not just live *with* strangers, they lived *among* them, and this generalized the dilemmas Simmel saw the stranger pose and generated fresh challenges for the practice of social, economic, and political life.

Rapid population growth, often extending over decades, was not unknown in early modern Asia or Europe. Yet it was always checked and often reversed by epidemics, famines, wars, and natural catastrophes. It was Malthus's genius to discover this pattern in his *Essay on the Principle of Population*, first published in 1798. The cyclical nature of premodern populations meant that in aggregate terms no continent in the world is estimated to have exceeded a compounded annual rate of growth of 0.08 percent before 1750. And yet, as Malthus was writing, Britain was defying the pattern and sustaining the rapid growth of a population on a hitherto unimaginable scale, reaching a peak of 1.6 percent annual growth in the decade after 1811 (or 1.8 percent for England and Wales). This peak should not obscure the long and sustained pattern of population growth: between the 1780s and the 1840s Britain's annual growth did not fall below 1 percent and then did so only because of the famine in Ireland. England and Wales sustained a 1 percent growth rate between 1780 and 1900. Effectively, the population doubled in size during both halves of the nineteenth century. At the advent of the twentieth century, Britain's population was almost four times larger than it had been in the middle of the eighteenth century.

Britain's population had not just been the first to break through the Malthusian trap; its growth was *rapid* as well as *sustained*. Its rate of growth was faster than any other European nation. Between 1800 and

1913 the number of Britons quadrupled, while Russia's population tripled in size, Italy and Spain's doubled, and France's rose by barely 50 percent. Even though France's population had been almost double the size of Britain's in 1800, it was surpassed by 1900.[18] With only 5.7 percent of Europe's land-mass, Britain's population as a percentage of the total European population (which was itself increasing at unprecedented rates) rose from 7.6 percent in 1680 to 15.1 percent in 1900.[19] Britain's population surge was no less impressive compared to its potentially biggest rivals China and the United States of America (see figure 1). China, for whom we lack reliable data, especially after 1851, continued to exemplify a classic early modern pattern, its population rising and falling until its growth was sustained from the late nineteenth century. Only America's population was growing faster, at more than 3 percent annually until the 1860s before falling to 2.2 percent in the first decade of the twentieth century; rising from a recorded 3.9 million in 1790 to 23.3 million in 1850 and 92.4 million by 1910. This phenomenal surge of people was made possible partly by slavery and immigration. Although the experience of rapid and sustained population growth was replicated by many societies in the late nineteenth century, many more did not experience it until the twentieth century. Thus while the world's annual rate of population growth between 1750 and 1950 was a remarkable 0.59 percent, after 1950 it reached a staggering 1.75 percent.[20]

Britain became a society of strangers not just by dint of the rapid and sustained growth of its population but because of its increasingly urban form. By 1871 Britain was the first predominantly urban society in the world.[21] No other society in human history had experienced this scale of urbanization. France and America (like Russia and Japan) did not reach 50 percent urbanization until the mid-twentieth century, and China not until the end of the century (see figure 2). And the size of Britain's cities, especially London, left all others in its wake: by 1880 London was the world's largest city by some distance (it was the size of Paris, New York, Tokyo, Beijing, and Mexico City *combined*). Thereafter, the rest of the world played catch-up, quickly. Whereas in 1750 there

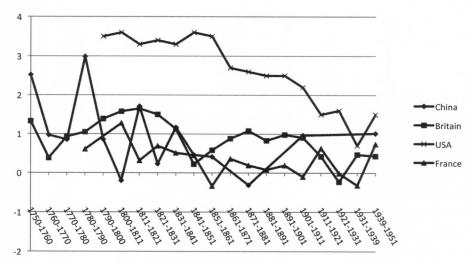

Figure 1. Comparative Rates of Population Growth.

Source: Chen-Siang Chen, "Population Growth and Urbanization in China, 1953–1970," *Geographical Review*, 63, 1 (January 1973), 55–72; John D. Durand, "The Population Statistics of China, A.D. 2–1953," *Population Studies*, 13, 3 (March 1960), 209–56; B.R. Mitchell, *British Historical Statistics* (Cambridge: Cambridge University Press, 1988; idem, *International Historical Statistics: Europe, 1750–2005* (New York: Palgrave Macmillan, 2007); U.S. Department of the Census, *Historical Statistics of the United States, Colonial Times to 1957.* Statistical Abstract Supplement.

were only three cities with more than 500,000 inhabitants in the world and they were all in Europe (London, Paris, Constantinople), by 1900 there were eleven cities double that size— six in Europe (Berlin, Constantinople [renamed Istanbul in 1830], Leningrad, London, Paris, Vienna), three in North America (New York, Chicago, and Philadelphia), two in Asia (Tokyo, Calcutta). A century later there were twenty-eight cities with populations of more than 4 million (the size of London in the 1870s) in Asia, eleven in North America, four in South America, and three in Europe.[22] Only 13 percent of the world's population had been urbanized in 1900 (up a mere 4 percent from 1600), yet by 1950 that

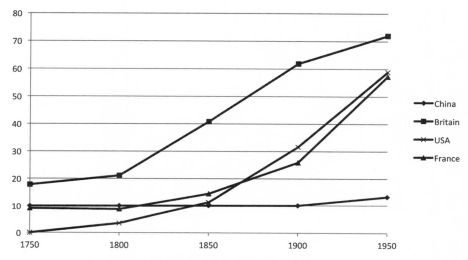

Figure 2. Comparative Percentage of Urban Populations.

Source: Chen-Siang Chen, "Population Growth and Urbanization in China, 1953–1970," *Geographical Review,* 63, 1 (January 1973), 55–72; Jan de Vries, *European Urbanization* (Cambridge, MA: Harvard University Press, 1984); Bernard Lepetit, "Patterns of Settlement," in Akira Hayami, Jan de Vries, and Ad van der Woude (eds.), *Urbanization in History: A Process of Dynamic Interactions* (Oxford: Clarendon Press, 1990); B. R. Mitchell, *British Historical Statistics* (Cambridge: Cambridge University Press, 1988); idem, *International Historical Statistics: Europe, 1750–2005* (New York: Palgrave Macmillan, 2007); U.S. Department of the Census, *Historical Statistics of the United States, Colonial Times to 1957.* Statistical Abstract Supplement.

figure had climbed to 29 percent and almost reached 50 percent in 2005 (as Britain had done a century and a half earlier).[23]

Because the British Isles were a relatively small land-mass, the increasing size and urban concentration of the population gave it an unprecedented density, a trend even more apparent when we consider the vast majority of Britain's population lived in England and Wales. Despite the rapidity of its growth, the total population of England and Wales was about as densely concentrated as France's until 1800, while

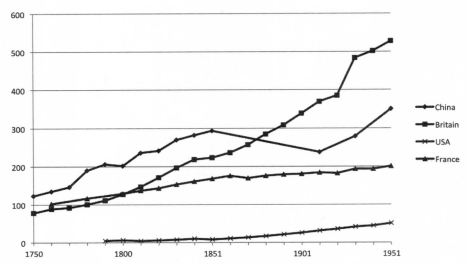

Figure 3. Comparative Population Density (people per square mile).

Source: John D. Durand, "The Population Statistics of China, A.D. 2–1953," *Population Studies*, 13, 3 (March 1960), 250; B.R. Mitchell, *British Historical Statistics* (Cambridge: Cambridge University Press, 1988), 7; idem, *International Historical Statistics: Europe, 1750–2005* (New York: Palgrave Macmillan, 2007), 4.

China's continued to outstrip it until the 1840s (see figure 3). It was in the second half of the nineteenth century that the density of Britons in England and Wales became most strikingly apparent. Although China and the United States (like Russia) then had larger populations than Britain, the enormous and expanding landmasses of these countries ensured that their populations remained more dispersed. According to the calculations of *The British Dominions Yearbook*, by 1918 only Eygpt's Nile Valley and Belgium had more people per square mile than England and Wales. Although Java and the Netherlands were in sight, the next most concentrated population was in Japan, where there were 324 people per square mile compared to 592 in England and Wales.[24]

The final ingredient for making Britain a society of strangers was the increasing mobility of its population over greater distances. Initially, as we shall see, urbanization was primarily the product of relatively short migrations; people usually traveled to nearby cities from the surrounding countryside. Nonetheless, the reach and scale of mobility was radically extended between the middle of the eighteenth and the middle of the nineteenth century when a revolution in transportation bequeathed Britons a radically improved road system, a railway network, and steam ships. The transport revolution greatly facilitated the flow of people as well as goods around and beyond the nation. By 1873 Jules Verne's character Phileas Fogg believed that new rail routes, navigation networks, and steam ships made it possible to travel around the world in just eighty days. No wonder that in his *Expansion of England* (1883) the imperial historian John Seeley declared that "in the modern world distance has very much lost its effect."[25] Even though extranational migration was a general European phenomenon; more migrants left Britain than any other European nation between 1815 and 1930, accounting for 36 percent of all of Europe's migrants. Many of these migrants were destined for the so-called white settler colonies of Canada, Australia, New Zealand, and South Africa but by 1919 the British Empire stretched over a quarter of the globe and included almost a third of the world's population, an estimated 458 million people spread across 13 million square miles. The United States also remained an integral part of the broader British world and continued to attract the majority of Britain's emigrants throughout the nineteenth century. The English-speaking Anglo world created by Britain's emigrants "grew over sixteenfold in 1790–1930, from around 12 million to around 200 million—a far greater rate than Indian and Chinese growth, as well as Russian and Hispanic."[26]

There is, then, good evidence to suggest that the sustained and rapid growth of a population that was increasingly mobile over ever-greater distances made Britain the first to experience the new social condition of modernity, namely living in a society of strangers. Although new forms of abstraction were used to reimagine and reorganize the practice of political, economic, and social life beyond the local and personal, these were neither new nor unique to Britain. They had been anticipated by the Enlightenments of the East, especially those that had informed the imperial Chinese system of government, and were further developed in Enlightened Europe and put to use by the revolutionary nation-states of the United States and France to establish new forms of government and legitimacy.[27] Although a new nation-state was forged in Britain after the revolution of 1688 and the Act of Union with Scotland in 1707, it was the increasing size and mobility of the population, and the extending reach of its imperial polity, that made the application of new techniques of abstraction especially urgent and potent.

New rules of social engagement and more elaborate forms of social classification were codified so that strangers could size up and navigate each other on the street, in the railway carriage, or in the matrimonial advert. In this new society of strangers, power and authority could no longer reside solely in individuals made conspicuously visible through ceremonies and tours. Instead we will see how in Britain's expanding imperial state it was gradually relocated to abstract and anonymous bureaucratic systems that were transferable across vast distances. Civil society was also transformed in the mirror image of the modern forms of state power it sought to contest and contain. Those in political movement built organizations that made it possible for people across the nation and empire to imagine sharing interests and even rights with distant strangers. Similarly, economic transactions long embedded in local networks and personal relations of credit and trust were increasingly restructured around new abstract and standardized systems of exchange.

For sure, this process of abstraction was gradual and uneven, but it was also dialectical. That is to say it generated a countermovement of attempts to reembed social, political, and economic relations in the local and personal. We will see how in each of these areas the society of strangers posed a quite different set of problems. As various forms of abstraction were used to address these problems, they invariably generated fresh challenges that then animated attempts to reembed them. It was a process that highlights how trust had to be built in the new systems and practices around which the modern world was reorganized if they were to endure. Thus, to provide some obvious examples: new centralized, bureaucratic systems of state power encouraged the rediscovery of the local parish as the essential unit of government; charismatic leaders thrived in bureaucratic political organizations; and the factory system of production spawned a highly personalized and paternal style of management. Historians have often mistaken these phenomena as evidence of the survival of tradition—either as the stubborn grip of the *ancien regime* or an alternative set of values and practices used to resist the modern—rather than as attempts to localize and personalize new abstract systems.[28] Instead of a simple process of change and continuity, transformation and resistance, this dialectic of abstraction and reembedding occurred simultaneously and was mutually constitutive.

Not even a very long book could comprehensively map how the society of strangers and the dialectic of abstraction and reembedding it unleashed made Britain modern. Instead, *Distant Strangers* proceeds through case studies that seek to illuminate how the realms of society, economy, and polity were restructured and reimagined. This helps illuminate how a new conceptual understanding of society, economy, and polity as not just their own discrete domains but as systems, with their own rhythms and forms of organization that required standardized rules and practices. Indeed, so reified did the understanding of those domains and their systems become that they were endowed with their own explanatory logics—so that history itself was seen to be driven by economic, social, and political laws. Each chapter then explores the remaking of economic, political, and social life while also defamiliarizing those *effects* of modernity we have often taken as its *causes*.

If this was how Britain became modern, when and where did it happen? A key intervention of the book is to suggest that Britain did not become modern in the eighteenth century as a consequence of the Glorious Revolution of 1688, the Industrial Revolution, or the Enlightenment.

As we have already seen, there were early modern precursors that anticipated the society of strangers and the abstraction of social, economic, and
political relations, but they worked on different scales and were rarely
sustained. My argument neither intends nor needs to provide a caricature of early modern societies as only rooted in local and personal relations where everyone knew each other. Indeed, frequently I return the
reader to the late seventeenth and early eighteenth centuries to trace the
processes of change that made Britain modern. Nonetheless, I am insist-
ent, some will find wearily so by the relentless flow of data, that, measured both qualitatively and quantitatively, the nineteenth century (and
more specifically the decades between 1830 and 1880) was the decisive
moment of Britain's great transformation.[29] There are those like Virginia
Wolfe with hubris enough to identify a particular moment, in her case
"on or about December 1910," when the world cracks and begins anew.
Historians are prone to do so by using revolutions—hence the ubiquity
of 1789—to demarcate the break between the early and late modern periods, but most recognize that even those dramatic events are part of longer
processes of change. Certainly Britain did not become modern in a single
decade, let alone a year, or month. The scale and nature of the great
transformation was palpable in the 1830s, but it was not until the 1880s and
often continuing deep in to the twentieth century that the new forms of
social, political, and economic organization were naturalized.

The important but not necessarily constitutive place of the British
Empire in that transformation will, I hope, become self-evident in the
following pages. Clearly I do not suggest that you need an empire to
become modern. Britain's imperial expansion played no part in the dramatic and sustained expansion of its domestic population. Nonetheless,
the flow of emigrants from Britain across the empire significantly
extended that population's mobility, while the size of the populations
and territories colonized generated new problems of governing over
and trading with distant strangers. Empire did not make Britain modern, even if the problems of governing distant strangers did make it a
laboratory for abstracting and then reembedding new forms of author-

ity. Although these were sometimes imported to Britain from the colonies, it was not a one-way street and the traffic flowed both ways.

Ultimately, I am less interested in whether Britain was the first modern society than whether this understanding of modernity is transferable and can be applied elsewhere without the same difficulties that plagued modernization theories that grounded their accounts in Enlightenment, industrialization, or revolution. My broader contention is that if modernity has any utility as an analytical category it must be to capture a singular condition—a shared historical process—albeit one with alternative trajectories and iterations. Think less of the many tributaries that lead to a river that flows inexorably to the sea and more of a freeway on which cars travel in both directions and one is never entirely sure where each car has come from or which exit they will take.

CHAPTER TWO

A Society of Strangers

In 1759 Adam Smith's *Theory of Moral Sentiments* suggested that because the emerging commercial society had generated an increasing number of transactions between strangers it would improve the morality of the population. Because we are more likely to behave badly in front of family and friends than we are with people we do not know, Smith argued that the old world structured around intimate local and personal relations could not provide the same discipline, restraint, and moral propriety that would be created by interactions with strangers. Acknowledging that the increasing mobility and complexity of commercial society would erode the affective ties of people and communities, he hoped that self-interest (our desire for strangers to see us as we would like to see ourselves) would provide a more effective source of moral opprobrium. The new commercial society of strangers Smith imagined in 1759 was the exception, not the rule; it existed only in a limited number of places and forms of trade, as *The Wealth of Nations* was at pains to point out nearly twenty years later.

By the end of the nineteenth century the founding fathers of sociology—Durkheim, Simmel, Tonnies, and Weber—all considered that living in a society of strangers was the defining feature of the modern condition. In different ways they all associated modernity with similar processes of social fragmentation and differentiation that increased the complexity of society. The rise of individualism, mobility, and urbanization had, they suggested, created a modern society of strangers characterized by anonymity and anomie. Although none of these interpreters of the social condition of modernity were British, in this chapter we shall see that Smith was right to identify that a new society of strangers began to emerge in Britain in the middle of the eighteenth century. Yet rather than pointing to new types of commercial relations, or to the process of industrialization, I suggest that it was rapid and sustained growth of a population that became increasingly mobile (over ever-greater distances) and urban in form that created a society of strangers by the middle of the nineteenth century. Although continental European social scientists did not theorize the modern nature of this social condition until the late nineteenth century, their predecessors in Britain had for decades been busily investigating the myriad new social problems generated by it or trying to catalogue strangers into recognizable social types.

THE GREAT TRANSFORMATION

The Reverend Thomas Malthus ensured that one of the chief claims to Britain being the first modern society was its ability to sustain rapid population growth. Writing during the late eighteenth and early nineteenth centuries, Malthus identified a structuring "principle of population" that had plagued all societies in human history: namely that population growth would always outstrip food supply and be checked by the miseries of want, disease, and famine. And yet, within decades of his death in 1834 it was apparent that Britain had escaped the so-called Malthusian trap and been able to sustain a population that had effectively doubled in size during the first half of the nineteenth century and has since never ceased to grow.

During the seventeenth century the population of England and Wales rose and fell in proper Malthusian fashion reaching a peak of

TABLE I

Population of the United Kingdom (millions)

	England and Wales	Scotland	Ireland	Total
1701	5.47			5.47
1751	6.47	1.27	3.12	10.9
1801	8.89	1.6	5.1	15.6
1851	17.93	2.89	6.55	27.4
1901	32.53	4.47	4.46	41.5
1951	43.76	5.09		48.9

SOURCE: B.R. Mitchell, *British Historical Statistics.* Cambridge: Cambridge University Press, 1988.

5.3 million in 1656 before receding to 4.9 million in 1686. All that changed during the eighteenth century when, even without the incorporation of Scotland (1707) and Ireland (1801), the population expanded significantly, and with them doubled in each half of the century (see table 1). If Malthus was alarmed by the rate of growth at the end of the eighteenth century he would have been horrified that the population of the newly United Kingdom almost doubled in size from 15.6 million to 27.4 (despite the famine in Ireland, which had made its growing population fall back by 1.6 million from the figures of 1841) between 1801 and 1851. The pace of growth barely slackened in the second half of the nineteenth century; by 1901 the population had reached 41.5 million. In a century and a half Britain's population had quadrupled in size.

How this happened, and why it happened first in Britain, has preoccupied historians and demographers for two centuries. The current orthodoxy reflects the labors of the Cambridge's Population History Group and plays down improvements in public health and epidemiology by suggesting that mortality rates declined slowly (life expectancy at birth rose from 31.8 to 41.3 between 1686 and 1871 before accelerating to 69.2 by 1950), and that the gross reproduction rate (i.e., the numbers of daughters a woman would have) only marginally increased from 2.17 to

2.54 between 1688 and 1871. Instead, reworking Malthus's later arguments, Cambridge's historical demographers have argued that families prudentially adapted their size in relation to wage levels: thus, the age of marriage for women fell from twenty-five to twenty-two between 1700 and 1850, while the average number of children in a family rose from 5.7 to 6.2 between 1771 and 1831. Whether the calculation of the cost and benefit of children was so centered on wage levels, however, seems disputable. We know from the debates about whether Britons' standards of living improved during industrialization that long-term macromeasurements of income are obscured not only by short-term economic fluctuations but profound differentials of geography, occupation, and gender as well as distinct regional patterns in the costs of food and rent.[1] And if population rose and fell only according to such purely economistic calculations, we remain at a loss to explain the phenomenal growth or relative stagnation of Russia's and France's predominantly rural populations during the nineteenth century.

Explanations of Britain's so-called demographic transition into fertility decline and reduced rates of population growth from the late nineteenth century provide a more nuanced account of how families made prudential calculations about their size. As the introduction of compulsory schooling prevented children from earning their keep as wage earners, the increased state regulation of child rearing reduced the prestige of parenting, and improved public health reduced infant mortality rates, people married later, and had fewer children. The average number of children born to a married woman fell dramatically from six to just over two during the span of the nineteenth century. It turns out that Malthus may have been wrong that population growth was unsustainable, but he was right that the key to its successful management lay with culture overcoming biology and allowing families to plan or try to manage their size through sexual abstinence and withdrawal during intercourse. And thanks to the constitutive role of culture in this process the general Euro-American process of rapid growth and stabilization masked subtle national variations with locally specific causes.[2] From this perspective the causes of Britain's rapid and sustained population growth may well have been multiple, not singular, and rooted as much in new cultural conceptions of the family and child as by wage levels or improvements in agricultural productivity or public health.

Whatever allowed Britain to break the Malthusian trap ensured that it became a very young country. By 1851, 60 percent of the population was less than twenty-four years old—a figure that fell only slightly to just more than 50 percent by 1901 despite the lengthening of life expectancy. And this youthful population was increasingly mobile. The 1851 census illustrated that 67 percent of those ages twenty to twenty-four were migrants in urban settings and 58 percent in the rural ones. Youth alone was not the only driver of mobility; the relaxation of the laws of settlement, intended to restrain the mobility of the poor by providing them relief only in their "home" parishes, was also critical. At the end of the seventeenth century these laws became more restrictive as the definition of settlement was confined to those who rented or owned property, paid taxes, held office, or had worked there for a year (women's rights were realized only at marriage). Only those with letters from their own parochial officers testifying to their good character were free to move between parishes. Nonetheless, as much as 65 percent of the population is estimated to have left their parishes between 1660 and 1730 in the quest for work or marriage. Much of this movement remained local, seasonal, and circular, with most individuals returning to their parishes of settlement. The majority of poor law settlement cases heard in Kent between 1723 and 1795 were for men who had traveled fewer than thirty-five miles, although there is evidence that one in seven moved beyond their counties of origin during this period.[3]

The weakening of the settlement laws in 1795 and 1834, the pull of the new urban centers, and the onset of the agricultural depression from the 1870s transformed this traditional pattern of predominantly short-range and seasonal migration. By 1851 only half of those living in London more than twenty years of age had been born there, while a third of Lancashire's inhabitants came from other counties, with the

Irish alone accounting for more than 10 percent of the total.[4] In other industrializing regions—Central Scotland, South Wales, and the West Midlands—a quarter of their populations had been born outside of the counties in which they lived. In industrializing cities like Glasgow and Manchester, more than half of the population were born elsewhere, and even Birmingham had a higher percentage of "foreigners" at 41 percent than did London at 38 percent.[5] This trend of internal migration over greater distances continued in the second half of the nineteenth century, no doubt fueled by the great flight from the countryside after the 1870s. By 1911, 36 percent of the population of England and Wales were living outside their native counties. Of course, old patterns of short-distance migration also continued. Two-thirds of rural migrants moved less than fifteen miles in 1851, so that in rural counties like Devon 82 percent of its population were born Devonians, and a further 8 percent had been born in neighboring counties.[6]

Much migration, both long and short distance, was to towns and cities where people continued to live largely transient lives. In the 1840s more than half of families in the London parishes of Westminster and St. George-in-the-East had lived in their homes for less than a year. Similarly, in Liverpool during the nineteenth century less than 20 percent of the population remained settled at the same address for a decade, while 40 percent moved within a single year—a figure confirmed by Booth's study of Bethnal Green in the 1880s.[7] Although we need much more research on this, it appears that it was not until the end of the nineteenth century—and the growth of public housing and owner-occupiers—that the British population began to become increasingly settled and attached to homes in particular places.[8]

Even though Britain had the earliest and most rapid, generalized, and sustained experience of urbanization in Europe (and arguably the world), its urban population grew upon a rural one whose size remained essentially static until the 1870s.[9] Throughout the eighteenth century, the growing population remained proportionately the same and predominantly rural, with only 20 percent living in towns by 1800, up just

2 percent from 1700, when six hundred to seven hundred towns, with populations between five hundred and one thousand, "were scattered across the nation like small islands amidst a sea of villages, hamlets and fields."[10] Despite the urban renaissance and the growth of London, eighteenth-century Britain remained a deeply rural society. Once again, the big change came in the nineteenth century. In 1801, 80 percent of the population of 15 million was rural; a century later, 80 percent of a population that had now reached 41 million was urban. The really dramatic shift came in the final quarter of the nineteenth century. In 1871, 50 percent of the population of 31.5 million remained rural, but by 1911 that figure had fallen precipitously to just 25 percent of 45 million—a loss of more than 7.5 million people from the countryside (with Scotland and Wales hit especially hard). Of course, when Britain became a predominantly urban population depends on your definition: it is 1851 if *urbanity* is defined by towns of 2,500 people, it is 1871 if that figure rises to 10,000, and 1901 if we take the measure of urban centers to be a population of 50,000.[11]

Whatever your measure, the galloping size of towns and cities was astounding. London was a juggernaut. Already in 1750 its population of 675,000 dwarfed all other cities, but by 1801 it had reached 1 million; by 1841, 2 million; by 1861, 3 million; by 1881, 4.7 million; by 1901, 6.5 million; and by 1931, 8.2 million. Throughout this dizzying expansion, which drew people from across the United Kingdom, London's inhabitants represented consistently around 15 percent of the population of England and Wales. No other city could compete with London's size, but other cities grew faster and sprang up within a couple of generations. By 1931, Manchester was ten times the size it had been in 1801 with its population increasing from 75,000 in 1801 to 339,000 by 1851; 645,000 by 1901; and 766,000 by 1931. Similar tenfold increases in the same time frame were evident for Birmingham, Liverpool, Glasgow, Belfast, Cardiff, Swansea, Gateshead, South Shields, Salford, Sheffield, Huddersfield, Blackburn, Bradford, Stoke, Wolverhampton, Hull, Leicester, Coventry, Derby, and Brighton. In 1811 only London had a population more than 100,000, whereas a century later 35 percent of the population lived in forty-one cities of that size. Although in the first half of the nineteenth century much of this migration into new urban centers came from the surrounding hinterland and counties, they also attracted migrants from across the country (see figure 4).[12]

Migration was also imperial in scope. England had long had a centrifugal pull for the Welsh and Scots looking for work, military service, or offices of state, but it was the calamity of the famine in Ireland that created the first mass colonial migration to the metropole. The size of the Irish population on the mainland nearly doubled in size between 1841 and 1861 when it reached more than 800,000. Despite these numbers and the arrival of around two hundred thousand Eastern European Jews in the late nineteenth century, migration to Britain remained negligible in scale until the 1950s. Emigration from Britain began with the exodus to North America, with some 350,000 people migrating there by 1700 and a further 750,000 joining them by 1800 (of whom 75 percent went unwillingly as convicts or indentured laborers). Between 1750 and 1939, an estimated 10 million emigrants left England and Wales, and a further 2.5 million from Scotland. Just in the decade before 1914, 1.7 million emigrants left Britain—more than double the numbers of Britons killed during the Great War.[13] These migrants spread across the British Empire and its white settler colonies as well as the broader British world that still included the most popular destination of the United States of America.

Intracolonial migration was also considerable, much of it forced. The British Empire was first built upon the institution of slavery. The plantation economies developed by white settlers in North America and the West Indies for the production of cotton, sugar, coffee, and cocoa sold to the expanding European markets depended upon importing slave labor from Africa and other forms of unfree (convict or indentured) labor from Britain itself. By 1750 there were 295,000 slaves in the Caribbean and a further 247,000 in North America—a fraction of the 3 million slaves brought to the Americas on British ships during the eighteenth century, half the total number of slaves transported.[14] In 1800 slaves accounted for 90 percent of the Caribbean's population and a

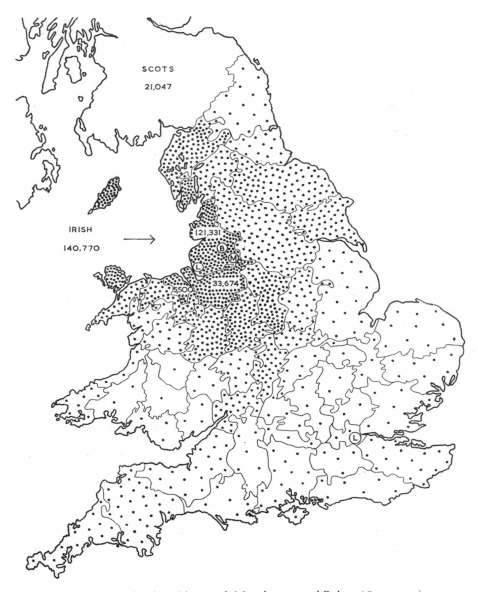

Figure 4. Migration into Liverpool, Manchester, and Bolton (1851 census).

Source: Arthur Redford, *Labour Migration in England, 1800–1850* (Manchester: Manchester University Press, 1926), app. E.

quarter of the inhabitants of British North America. The abolition of the slave trade by Britain in 1807 and the eventual emancipation of slaves across its empire in 1837 could not prevent a further 3 million slaves from being shipped from West Africa during the nineteenth century. What it did do was catalyze new systems of bonded and indentured labor to fill the gaps left by slaves, especially in plantation economies. Alongside the use of local indigenous populations as forced "coolie" labor in much of Asia, Africa, and Australasia, some 4 million Indians, Chinese, Malays, and Sinhalese were sent across the world as unfree laborers between the 1830s and the Great War. By the time indentured labor was eventually abolished in 1922, more than a million Indians had been scattered across the empire—in Southeast Asia, in eastern and southern Africa, the Caribbean, and the Pacific Islands.[15]

STRANGERS IN A SHRINKING WORLD

The ability of Britons to move around the nation, empire, and the world owed much to a revolution in transportation that helped collapse distance (and the time spent traveling it) in unprecedented ways. Canal and road building in the eighteenth century, as well as the advent of the railway and steam ship in the nineteenth century, made Britons increasingly mobile over greater distances and thus more likely to encounter and live among strangers.

The improvement of the roads came first from the military imperatives of the state. Following the Act of Union with Scotland in 1707, and the Jacobite rebellions of 1715 and 1745, military surveyors, engineers, and soldiers laid nine hundred miles of paved road linking Scotland's highland and lowland fortifications. The techniques of surveying, cutting embankments, and paving developed while building these roads diffused southward with the great boom of constructing turnpike roads from the 1750s as well as eventually to the roads maintained by local parishes. Between 1750 and 1772 more than 500 trusts were formed and constructed 15,000 miles of road (see figure 5a and b). Even so, when the

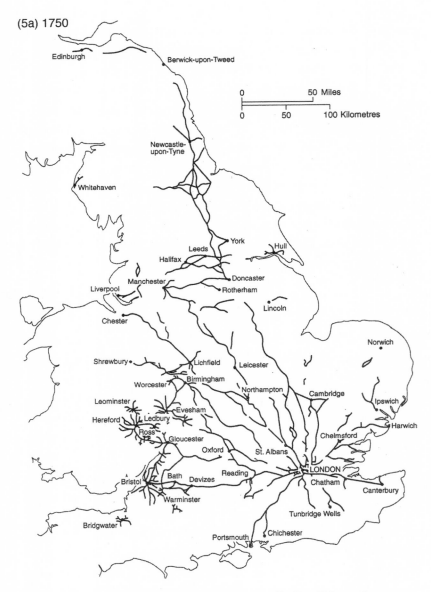

(5a) 1750

Figure 5a and b: The Development of the Turnpike Road Network, 1750
and 1770.

Source: Martin Daunton, *Progress and Poverty: An Economic and Social History of
Britain, 1700–1850* (Oxford: Oxford University Press, 1995), 300–303. Both from
E. Pawson, *Transport and Economy: The Turnpike Roads of Eighteenth Century
Britain* (London: Academic Press, 1977).

(5b) 1770

0   50 Miles
0   50   100 Kilometres

Berwick-upon-Tweed

Carlisle
Newcastle
Durham
Whitehaven
Stockton
Kendal

York
Leeds   Hull
Liverpool   Doncaster
Holyhead
Chester   Manchester   Sheffield
Newcastle   Lincoln
Nottingham
Shrewsbury
Leicester   Kings Lynn   Norwich
Aberystwyth
Birmingham
Coventry   Northampton   Cambridge
Worcester
Banbury   Ipswich
Brecon   Hereford
Gloucester   Harwich
Swansea   Monmouth   Oxford
Cardiff
Bristol   Reading   LONDON
Barnstaple   Canterbury
Bridgwater   Frome   Winchester   Dover
Salisbury
Southampton
Exeter   Portsmouth
Truro   Plymouth

government funded its own postal coaches in 1785, the General Post Office (GPO) deployed a team of surveyors to measure distances across the growing network and to map the lamentable quality of many road surfaces. Once again it was the military imperatives of the state, this time following the Act of Union with Ireland in 1801, that catalyzed further improvements with two state-funded trunk roads, stretching 1,700 miles, that connected England to Wales and Wales to Ireland (via Hollyhead), as well as improvements to the Great North Road between London and Edinburgh. With the Highways Act of 1835, the rest of the 120,000-mile road network, including the 98 percent maintained by more than 17,000 parishes and turnpike trusts, had to be maintained in accordance with central standards with smooth macadamized paving (named after McAdam, its engineer) mounded in the middle to assist drainage and set on a foundation of ten inches of gravel.[16]

As roads improved, Britain effectively shrank in size, and previously scattered and distant populations were forged into an increasingly closely knit national space. Already in 1715, eight hundred stagecoaches left London each week, but their intrepid travelers faced long and grueling journeys however short the distance. Even by the 1760s the London-to-Edinburgh coach ran once a month and could take up to two weeks. A century later all that had changed. The extension of the road network, the improved quality of road surfaces and stagecoach design, as well as the introduction of the GPO's faster mail coaches all greatly improved journey times (see figure 6). By the 1820s, 1,500 coaches left London each week, with 700 mail coaches and 3,300 privately operated stagecoaches forming a national network of road travel that traveled nearly four times faster than they had in the 1750s.

The arrival of the railway, with the iconic opening of the Manchester-to-Liverpool line in 1830, did not herald the end of horse-drawn coach travel by road. In the first place, the railway spread slowly. There were just five hundred miles of track in 1838, but the speculative frenzy in the 1840s ensured that by 1850 what John Ruskin described as the new "iron veins that traverse the frame of our country" were in place, with

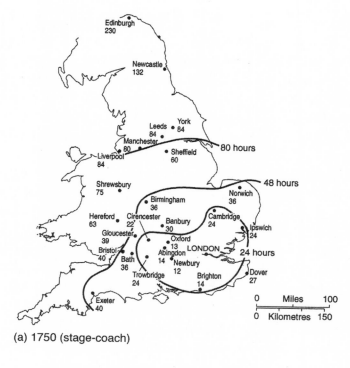

(a) 1750 (stage-coach)

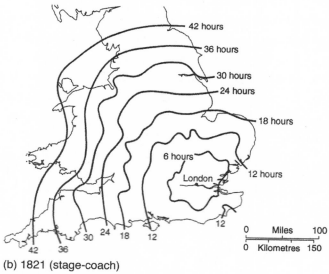

(b) 1821 (stage-coach)

Figure 6. The Gathering Speed of Road Travel by Stagecoach.

Source: Martin Daunton, *Progress and Poverty: An Economic and Social History of Britain, 1700–1850* (Oxford: Oxford University Press, 1995), 308.

six thousand miles connecting most of the nation's major towns. Some places—notably Cornwall, Wales, and the Scottish highlands—had to wait for the second half of the nineteenth century to be connected to the burgeoning railway network that extended across twenty-thousand miles by 1914 (see figure 7). Still, one in six localities lacked stations, and many remained dependent upon stagecoaches for travel to one— indeed, there were more than four times as many horses engaged in commercial passenger transport in 1901 than there had been in 1851. Even though the number of individual stagecoach journeys by road had peaked at 10 million in 1835, rail ushered in a new era of rapid mass transport. As early as 1845, 30 million journeys were made by rail, but the growth of the network and the reduction of ticket prices ensured that figure rose exponentially to 336.5 million by 1870. Third-class ticket passengers accounted for a third of that total in 1870, and by 1890 they represented two-thirds of railway passenger receipts. It was not just that more people were routinely traveling further distances by rail; they were doing so at unprecedented speeds. A journey from London to Manchester in 1845 took just six hours, and by 1910 the trip from London to Edinburgh by rail, which a century and a half earlier could at the very fastest take ten days, now lasted just ten hours. Distance had not been annihilated, but the increasing speed of travel had the effect of imaginatively shrinking it. (see figure 8). Although this clearly made Britons much more mobile over greater distances, we know remarkably little about what its consequences were for migration patterns. There is certainly evidence that population settlements grew along major rail lines, and cities like Middlesbrough were effectively created by the railway. When the Stockton and Darlington railway was extended to Middlesbrough, its population rose from just 40 people in 1821 to 7,631 in 1851. Most of those migrants came from the surrounding county of Yorkshire, but by 1871, when Middlesbrough had a population of 99,705, fewer than half came from Yorkshire.[17]

The railway did not just transform the experience of time and space in Britain; it brought the empire closer to home. When Phileas Fogg sat

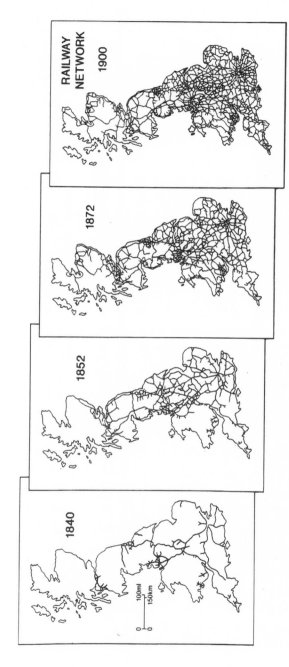

Figure 7. The Development of the Railway Network, 1840–1900.

Source: Nigel Thrift, "Transport and Communication, 1730–1914," in R. A. Dodgshon and R. A. Butlin (eds.), *An Historical Geography of England and Wales* (London: Academic Press, 1990), 462.

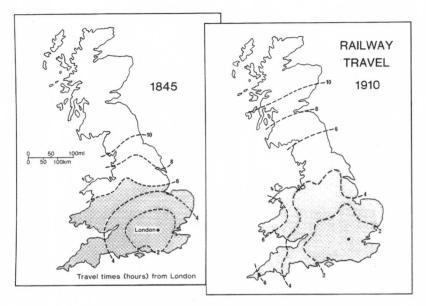

Figure 8. Railway Travel Times and Distance, 1845 and 1910.

Source: Nigel Thrift, "Transport and Communication, 1730–1914," in R. A. Dodgshon and R. A. Butlin (eds.), *An Historical Geography of England and Wales* (London: Academic Press, 1990), 462.

in London's Reform Club and wagered he could reach Calcutta in a mere twenty-three days and travel around the entire world in just eighty days, it was because of the news that the Rothal and Allahabad section of the Indian railway network had opened in 1872.[18] It was the colonial state that developed the railway in India, mindful of what Governor General Dalhousie (1848–56) described as the difficulties of governing the "vast extent of the empire." After the Revolt in 1857, more track was laid in the single year of 1858–59 than had existed previously; by 1865 the network included 3,500 miles of track; by the turn of the twentieth century it had grown to 25,100 miles; and by 1930 it was the third largest in the world at nearly 44,000 miles. Steam ships and better navigation routes were also a key part of Fogg's plan. In the early eighteenth century, the sea trip from London to Calcutta took anywhere between five and eight months depending upon the weather and prevailing winds. By the early nineteenth century, improved hull designs and better navigation systems took two months off that journey, but officials of the East India Company still had to wait at least half a year before receiving responses to their enquiries from London. The introduction of steam power, the use of lighter and more durable steel hulls, better maps, and navigation, as well as the opening of the Suez Canal in 1869, meant that Fogg's ambition of reaching Calcutta in twenty-three days was daring but doable.

The experience of traveling vast distances at unprecedented speeds meant that whether they migrated or not it became increasingly common for Britons to encounter strangers. The road and the railway in particular became new types of often disorientating and bewildering social spaces that had to be carefully navigated by learning new conventions of social interaction. From the middle of the eighteenth century, Britain's expanding road network was awash with soldiers, artisans, seasonal workers, preachers, entertainers (storytellers, ballad singers, fair workers, etc.), peddlers and tinkers, servants, state officials (excisemen, postal workers), and radical political leaders. These groups rarely used the road to get from *a* to *b*; more often they were part of regional circuits, with, for instance, Methodist preachers routinely walking between 150 and 250 miles of the same circuit every month and excisemen assigned 38-mile rural "rides" each day. Tramping was not the peripatetic ideal that the Romantic poets, the tightening of the vagrancy laws, and the advent of rail travel by the 1840s later made it. Far from a sublime experience of the pastoral, tramping was physically demanding and frequently dangerous. There was no better illustration of that than the fictional transformation, a century after his execution at the gallows in 1739, of the highway robber Dick Turpin from a violent criminal to a dashing and romantic figure. This fictional revival of highway robbery, like the discovery of India's murderous Thuggees at the same time, dramatized the continuing anxiety about the dangers of the road and the strangers encountered in transit.[19] The question of how to know whom one could trust became paramount. In the second half of the eighteenth century, trade associations and friendly societies were the first to develop regional tramping networks to welcome and support those identified as "brothers" or "friends."

Removed from the melee of those tramping the roads, the respectable middling sorts faced their own challenges, encountering strangers en masse at the imposing new depots and stations as well as the new intimacies of the coach and rail carriage. Coach travel was arduous: journeys were long, frequently too hot or too cold, and opportunities for refreshment, to stretch one's legs, or answer the calls of nature were limited. It was hard to maintain a polite distance from one's fellow passengers when they were tightly packed next to, or directly across from you, on bumpy roads. An advice literature quickly emerged to help guide travelers through the appropriate conventions of conversation and personal comportment, such as the proper parameters of small talk and the importance of avoiding unnecessary eye contact. "In no country in the world," a typical piece opined, "is the proportion of travelers to the population so great as in ours; and therefore it is peculiarly incumbent upon us to understand the morals of traveling."[20]

Trains were a little different, but although third-class passengers traveled like freight in open boxcars until 1844, first- and second-class passengers had carriages modeled on the U-style seating of the coach. Because the speed of rail travel made many who looked out of the windows nauseous, reading, which had been impossible in bumpy coach rides, became a way of avoiding eye contact and cultivating an appropriate detachment from one's fellow passengers. Book and news stalls quickly proliferated in railway stations. During the 1860s, two infamous murders on trains rang the death knell for the old coach style carriage as private compartments shared with potentially murderous strangers were no longer considered safe. After experimenting with "peep holes" between compartments and footboards outside the trains, rail carriages were redesigned around a connecting side corridor with sliding doors into each cabin. This also enabled passengers to walk around and have access to bathrooms.[21] From the 1860s, a new generation of urban travel developed for the respectable commuting suburban classes with the horse-drawn omnibus, the tram, and the underground "tube" in London. With shorter journeys and a more promiscuous social mix of passengers, carriage design followed the more open and fluid design of the lower-class rail coach where travelers were often forced to stand in close proximity to strangers. These forms of travel generated their own anxieties about pickpockets and the maintenance of personal space to avoid unwanted conversation and physical contact with strangers or their germs.[22]

MAKING SENSE OF THE SOCIETY OF STRANGERS

Above all, it was the city and its streets where the increasingly ubiquitous encounter with strangers was evident. London was the classic and earliest case, and guides to the City, like Ned Ward's *The London Spy* (1698–1700) or John Gay's poem *Trivia; or, The Art of Walking the Streets of London* (1716), began to appear from the late seventeenth century, although their numbers proliferated a century later when city directories also began to flourish. *The London Spy* quickly became canonical and established a genre in which local knowledge of the City's pleasures, treasures, mysteries, and dangers was provided for what Ward artfully described as the "mobility." Moving around the streets with their discordant sounds, multiple odors, and endless streams of people required learning the conventions of how to conduct oneself safely and respectably. City guides and etiquette manuals reminded the curious not to stare at strangers or look into private houses, to keep to the left when walking, and not to push or jostle in a crowd. One had to learn to become part of a crowd of strangers.[23] Physical actions that individuated one—like pushing, urinating, or spitting—were frowned upon. The coffee houses and pleasure gardens of eighteenth-century London were notorious laboratories for establishing the rules of polite and commercial sociability. The infamous "Macaroni Affray" at Vauxhall

Pleasure Gardens in 1773—when two gentlemen ended up challenging each other to a duel over the appropriate forms of polite exchange between men and women—shows how those rules of etiquette were slowly established by trial and error.[24]

Nonetheless, men of letters routinely remarked on the overwhelming size and anonymity of the City in the early nineteenth century. Frequently evoking the sense of bewilderment at the mass of humanity, they used aqueous metaphors of flows, torrents, and streams to capture its volume and sense of continuous movement. Wordsworth's account of his visit to London's "moving pageant" in the "Prelude" (1804–5) is often described as the first and an exemplary statement of the anomie of modern urban life. Although twenty years later Hazlitt, like Wordsworth, recognized the oddity of living in a city where even next-door neighbors did not know each others' names, he found it less alienating.[25] For Thomas de Quincey it was impossible to be as lonely as someone first encountering the anonymity of London's streets "in the centre of faces never-ending, without voice or utterance for him; eyes innumerable, that have 'no speculation' in their orbs which he can understand; and hurrying figures of men and women weaving to and fro, with no apparent purposes intelligible to a stranger...."[26] Because few streets had signs or names, and still fewer houses had numbers until the middle of the nineteenth century, navigating London often required trusting strangers for their local knowledge. Increasingly, guides—like W. G. Perry's tellingly titled *London Guide and Strangers' Safeguard against the Cheats, Swindlers, and Pickpockets that Abound ...* (1818)—warned the mobility to be wary whom they trusted for directions as they were easy prey to tricksters, swindlers, and imposters. Trusting strangers was a hazardous affair. Just as Moll Flanders discovered, pickpockets and prostitutes could pass as fashionably dressed ladies; a policeman wryly observed in one of G. W. M. Reynolds's *Mysteries* stories, "If we took up all persons that we know to be imposters, we should have half of London in custody."[27] By the late nineteenth century, even city inspectors and policemen went "undercover" to conduct their investigations, to say nothing of journalists and philanthropists "slumming" as members of the urban poor to experience poverty firsthand. In an environment where one was never sure who a stranger was, let alone whether he or she could be trusted, fears of fraud, crime, and sexual danger easily propagated. Men in search of sex with other men were victims of blackmailing scams that threatened to engulf them in scandal and the loss of their carefully cultivated reputations. Women shopping in a West End designed to make the streets respectable and safe fell prey to the unwanted attentions of men mistaking them as prostitutes. City periodicals and advice literature recommended that if women had to go unchaperoned during the day they could avoid being harassed by walking purposively rather than lingering at shop windows or bus stops and never returning a man's gaze or greeting.[28]

Because imposters were everywhere and could not be reliably identified by location or dress, new forms of expertise gathered around the classification and delineation of urban types. From the 1840s, representations of urban types and characters within the dark and dangerous labyrinth of the city stretched across high and low literary genres as well as the nascent social sciences. G. W. M. Reynolds's reputation as "the most popular writer in England" was largely built upon the enormous success of his *Mysteries of London,* which sold a stunning forty thousand copies a week from 1844. Reynolds's juxtaposition of the lives and vices of the rich and poor through a series of vignettes proved hugely influential and—like Dickens's novels or, later, Conan Doyle's Sherlock Holmes stories—provided an archeology of urban places and social types through the close observation of character. Of course, some of these attempts to grapple with and navigate the society of strangers in print—like etiquette books and urban guides—had been anticipated in the early modern print cultures of Europe and Asia, but only in part and only episodically. Such was the case in eighteenth-century London. Yet the proliferation of print culture and the unprecedented size of London in the nineteenth century ensured that there was a new intensity and scale to attempts to read and delineate strangers as knowable types. This was also apparent in visual culture. At the same mid-century moment, artists like William Powell Firth, William Maw Egley, and George Elgar Hicks became intensely focused upon the anonymous nature of urban life, especially at busy sites of social interaction like the General Post Office or Paddington Station. Egley's *Ominbus Life in London* (1859) captures the genre well (see figure 9). Its vivid portrayal of a densely packed omnibus that still more passengers hope to board lays out a whole series of different social types and illustrates the essential awkwardness of modern life. The viewer, like the inhabitants of the omnibus, not only learns that talking and staring at strangers is impolite but is encouraged to speculate on the moral character of the strangers assembled in such indelicately crowded company.[29]

We can understand the work of the emergent social sciences in the second half of that century as a culmination of these attempts to make the society of strangers legible through identifying collectivities—of race and classes—with distinct characteristics and locations. Henry Mayhew's portrayal of the "wandering tribes" that made up London's street life, first serialized in the *Morning Chronicle* from 1849, delineated "criminal classes" by dress, language, and physiognomy so that others could avoid them: "They are all," he wrote, "more or less distinguished for their high cheek-bones and protruding jaws—for their use of a slang language—for their lax ideas of property—for their general improvidence—their repugnance to continuous labour—their disregard of female honour—their love of cruelty—their pugnacity—and their utter want of religion." It was not such a large leap from Mayhew to Francis Galton's experiments developing composite photographs of criminal types from the 1870s.[30] Whereas social theorists on Europe's continent sought to imagine the deep structures that bound strangers together as a society, Britain's early social scientists of the social focused on the investigation and delineation of difference.

In the seventeenth and eighteenth centuries, various forms of social description and distinction had multiplied in a morass of ranks and orders, stations and degrees, sorts and classes. Gregory King's influential

Stamped Edition, 6d.

THE ILLUSTRATED LONDON NEWS.

No. 978—VOL. XXXIV.]   SATURDAY, JUNE 11, 1859.   [WITH A SUPPLEMENT, FIVEPENCE

"OMNIBUS LIFE IN LONDON."—FROM A PICTURE BY W. M. EGLEY.—IN THE BRITISH INSTITUTION.—SEE SUPPLEMENT, PAGE 571.

Figure 9. Omnibus Life in London.

Source: *Illustrated London News,* June 11, 1859.

studies of the population after 1688 deployed an elaborate list of more than twenty groups differentiated by "ranks, degrees, titles and qualifications." King's classifications—a jumble of political offices and qualification, social ranks and titles, and economic occupations—evaded precise definition but evoked an order in which everyone knew her or his proper role and place in a finely grained and unshakeable hierarchy.[31] By the early nineteenth century this made little sense. It was not just that maintaining and describing such an elaborate hierarchy of small differences was less possible in a society of strangers but that the intensifying work of social description created a new sense of society as its own domain that required its own forms of classification and distinction.

Before the late eighteenth century, when zoologists first used *society* to represent a distinct system of social organization in animals, the term had denoted a specific set of affiliations. This idea of society as a distinct realm—separate from politics and economy—was applied to the human condition only in the early nineteenth century. With gathering pace from the 1830s a plethora of work by journalists, statisticians, medics, philanthropists, employers, and politicians investigated "the condition of England," namely the seemingly deleterious effects of industrialization and urbanization upon the laboring poor. Despite their very different methods, approaches, genres, and politics, their work cumulatively established the social as a distinct area of enquiry with its own rhythms, questions, and problems that were quite separate from those of the economy or politics. Yet this idea of the social as an autonomous system, whose rhythms and laws could be discerned through the study of particular problems and questions, developed slowly. It was less evident in the work of the Social Science Research Association (1857 and 1886) than in Herbert Spencer's *The Study of Sociology* (1873), which drew upon evolutionary biology to conceptualize society as an organic and increasingly complex system, and Henry Maine's *Village-Communities in the East and West* (1876), which valorized the local and patriarchal ties that bound together "traditional" society. Even when the academic discipline of sociology formally and belatedly arrived in Britain with the formation of the Sociological Society in 1903, it remained less concerned with identifying iron laws of social development than in addressing specific social problems and describing and classifying social difference.[32] In contrast, continental sociologists, observing the newfound density and anonymity of French, German, and Italian cities, sought to understand the collective attributes and mentalities of the undifferentiated urban "crowd."[33]

The cultural work of the emergent social sciences in Britain was to make the society of strangers legible first by delineating the types of difference that structured its complexity and then to imagine ties that bound it together as a discrete system. Unsurprisingly, in the imperial nation that was Britain, social explorers and investigators turned to categories of race, not class, to understand the social problem of poverty in the world's largest and richest city. They did not have to travel far to discover *How the Poor Live,* for as George Sim found in 1883, it was "a dark continent within easy walking distance of the General Post Office." The poor were increasingly conceived less as a separate class than as a race apart and were frequently equated to "primitive" and "savage" peoples across the empire, with London's East End standing proxy for the dark continents of the East or Africa.[34] This racialization of the poor at home was intimately related to hardening ideas about racial difference across the empire following the Revolt in India (1857) and the rebellion in Jamaica's Morant Bay (1866). The primitive nature of London's poor and Britain's imperial subjects was rooted in the racial difference of their populations, which was increasingly explained not by culture and history but by an immutable biology. As Galton was experimenting with composite photographs of criminal types he was also developing the science of eugenics. Even Charles Booth's more statistically minded mapping of poverty in London categorized each street by the relative wealth of its inhabitants on a scale with yellow representing the highest "upper-middle and upper classes" and, of course, black signifying the "lowest class," which was further classified as "vicious, semi-criminal." Try as he might, Booth's classifications remained marked by the view of the poor as a race apart.[35] When class did appear as a way of conceiving the social order it was not the product of a sociological imagination but of the language of politics. Even then, despite Marx's long exile in Britain, the category of class remained frequently marginal and primarily understood in political, not social, terms as a relationship to the state and citizenship.[36] It was not until social scientists documented the expansion of the middle classes (in new technical forms of work, new housing estates, new leisure pursuits) and the erosion of traditional working-class communities and culture (by Americanized mass culture, urban planning, and eventually rising standards of living) between the 1930s and 1960s that class categories were eventually naturalized. In that sense class was most apparent at the moment of its dissolution or reshaping.[37]

RECONSTITUTING THE PERSONAL

Just as the society of strangers produced new conventions of behavior and ways of reading and understanding social difference, so it provided the conditions for the reconstitution of the intimate domain of personal relations. Nowhere was this more apparent than in the transformation of family life. There are disagreements about when and how the modern, nuclear family emerged, but few dispute that the extended corporate household, rooted in a broad kinship network, was eventually displaced by a family unit built around monogamous marriage and offspring who enabled the accumulation and transmission of property and wealth.[38] The rapid expansion and increasing mobility of the population seems to have sustained remarkably flexible forms of family and household life. In 1851 only 36 percent of households contained only conjugal family members of a married couple and their children, whereas "44% contained at least one extra person a lodger, servant or living in employee, visitor or relative."[39] Although the average size of households remained at around five between 1750 and 1850 before falling to a little more than three in 1950, there were significant variations across town and country and between occupations and classes. In Davidoff and Hall's sample of middle-class families, they note that the average household size in 1851 was a little more than six and rose to more than seven and fell closer to five at the upper and lower ends of that social spectrum. Larger groups also predominated among trade households where apprentices and shopmen were common, as well as among lower professional ones like teachers, which often included children resident in their schools. Moreover, the declining size of households elided their changing constituents, which, in 1850 included, besides kith and extended kin (nieces, nephews, cousins, and siblings), visitors, employees (including servants and apprentices), and lodgers. John Gillis has aptly described this type of household as "the family of strangers."[40]

It was only in the early twentieth century that the household became coterminous with the nuclear family. By the 1880s kith and kin had been largely jettisoned, and the average number of children had fallen from six to two in the space of two generations. Even so, family sizes still varied along a scale of 0–10 children in roughly equal proportions. In contrast, by the 1920s the overwhelming majority of families had between one and three children. As the size and composition of families changed, so did their economies of affection. Children became more closely bonded to their parents who, like their offspring, now lived far longer. The numbers of children who could expect to lose at least one parent declined sharply from 20 percent in 1741 to just 3 percent two hundred years later. As the surge of the population and its domestic migration into cities had largely subsided by the 1920s, this dwindling family unit with longer life expectancy was often both more settled and more isolated from the extended family.[41]

The affective relations of the nuclear family depended upon a new division of labor and regimes of privacy that shielded it from the society of strangers. Firstly, the family home became insulated from the world of paid work. The household had long been a site of work, with living spaces distributed around or on top of shops or workshops until the late eighteenth century, when many forms of production began to shift to factories and workshops and those in trade, retail, and the professions moved into separate, purpose-built shops and offices. Slowly, as a consequence, the commute to work was born as separate residential, commercial, and industrial areas began to emerge in the expanding urban areas. This was a cultural as much as economic process. At its heart lay the attempt to remove women and children from what was increasingly considered to be the masculine world of work. Men were supposed to financially support those now considered dependent upon his labor—his wife and the children she was expected to raise. Of course, for many, especially but not exclusively the working classes, this ideal was rarely achieved, because households remained dependent upon the skills or multiple incomes of all family members. Nonetheless, despite this unevenness, the ideal family cultivated a new privacy and distance from those strangers beyond the front door, shielding itself behind curtains, hedges, walls, gates, and drives.[42]

The emotional economy of family life was transformed in this new private space of the home. No longer considered contributors to the household economy, women and children became the objects of renewed emotional investment in a series of new family rituals such as the formalization of family meals, bedtime stories, holidays, and the celebration of birthdays.[43] Ironically this often relied upon physical detachment and distance between family members. When possible, children were removed to their own bedrooms, even though in 1911 three-quarters of families still lived in households with just one or two rooms. Upper-class children had always spent more time with servants than parents, but from the 1850s the middle classes also began to send their sons away to boarding schools. Forty-one new boarding schools were created between 1840 and 1869, and by the 1930s their numbers had reached around two hundred. Many of these schools served distinct regional communities, but even these had children whose parents were spread across the country and the empire. Indeed, for colonial officials sending their children to school in Blighty was a way of maintaining social status as well as Englishness.[44] By 1880, when elementary education became compulsory for all children, even the working class was forced to send their children to be taught by strangers at the local school.

Indeed the distance over which a family was spread became a marker of its respectability. Just as boys were scattered by their schooling, the middle-class marriage market, so critical for the raising of capital in family businesses, ensured that girls also often settled and raised families far from home. Letter writing enabled conjugal families to stay in touch, and the arrival of a letter was in and of itself symbolically important immaterial of the news it conveyed. As the speed of the domestic postal service improved and a flat-rate charge was introduced regardless of distance in 1839, familial communication became commercialized by greeting cards (that marked birthdays and holidays, Valentine's Day, or invitations to weddings and funerals) and the exchange of gifts that helped bind extended and distant relations into the intimate rhythms of family life. By the 1860s, even inhabitants in poor working-class districts with high levels of illiteracy like Oldham were receiving six letters a head. Similarly, the growing interest in family trees and genealogical research from the late nineteenth century, once the preserve of the aristocracy, typified a determination to make scattered families whole again and at the very least inscribe them in the family Bible.[45] Writing to pull the family together was especially critical for empire families who were always mobile and frequently separated. The rotation of offices within colonies and across continents, the use of periodic returns to the mother country on furloughs, the education of children in boarding schools, and summer residences in hill stations all served to separate husbands and wives, parents and children. In these conditions, when sons might not see their parents or siblings for years, letter writing was *the* form of exchange in the family's emotional economy and a key duty for mothers. It was an experience horribly generalized for many families during the Great War.[46]

Nowhere was the recrafting of intimate relations in a society of strangers more evident than in the rise of the matrimonial advertisements and personal columns. At least twenty-two matrimonial papers carrying these adverts were established in England between 1870 and 1914. Sold in newsstands and shops, they generally published between two hundred and five hundred adverts a week, with one editor extravagantly boasting that he was responsible for more than a thousand marriages a year. These publications sought to connect strangers in calculated ways and were aimed primarily at the lower middle classes of clerks and tradesmen who lacked the resources or familial connections to personally arrange a marriage and for whom a chance encounter or courtship appeared dangerous and unrespectable.[47] Similarly, although what we now know as "lonely heart" adverts had made daring appearances in the popular press since the 1860s, it became formalized as the personal column in 1915 when a magazine called the *Link* began publishing what its editor described as a new "social medium" devoted to those in pursuit of friendship and love, not marriage.[48] The old forms of courtship and marriage by no means disappeared, but they were supplemented by these new anonymous forms made necessary by, and only possible in, a society of strangers.

Just as the family developed new affective economies that allowed privacy from strangers outside the front door and intimacy between its increasingly scattered members, the increasingly performative nature of selfhood may have been a response to the anonymity of a social world increasingly populated by strangers. I am certainly not suggesting that the modern idea of the person as an individuated and autonomous self was a product of the society of strangers. We know that this new understanding of the self emerged during the seventeenth and eighteenth centuries. Its key ingredient was the shift from external points of reference for self-examination and direction, like the Protestant quest for individual salvation or the sublimation of the individual within a larger corporate body, to internal ones that recognized that every person was the master of his own knowledge (Descartes) and architect of his own life (Locke). Where once self-centeredness had appeared morally dubious or even sinful, it was slowly accepted and encouraged. This was evident in the mirrors, watches, and private bedrooms of the bourgeois home, in the new practices of self-reflection and introspection, in the emergence of the novel and its stories about individuated characters, in the proliferation of new creeds that posited the gendered individual as a bearer of political rights and celebrated the self-interested pursuit of wealth, and the development of new romantic ideas of the child and childhood as a uniquely formative moment of self-realization and education.[49] All provided new avenues of self-discovery and realization of a self that was taken as the essential core of an individual, and all developed independently of the increasing size, mobility, and anonymity of the population.

What was new and associated with the anonymity of modern life was the culture of performance that increasingly attended the tasks of crafting and projecting the self. There were those who rejected the new emphasis on interiority, intimacy, and authenticity and instead deliberately cultivated forms of selfhood predicated upon a stylized exterior and the maintenance of distance from others. The masquerade ball, so fashionable during the second half of the eighteenth century, can be understood in these terms as a stage for the performance of the self in a crowd of strangers.[50] If this understanding of selfhood reached its apogee with "the dandy," it was by no means the preserve of elite figures. Although Beau Brummell and Oscar Wilde at the start and end of the nineteenth century respectively remained its chief exemplars, late Victorian music halls were replete with "Champagne Charlies" and "swells" playfully performing different social identities both on and off stage.[51] Even the quest for an authentic interiority spawned a variety of practices for the public performance of self-realization, its discovery and enactment. Narratives of conversion, of the birth of a new self, became staples of Methodist literature and were soon reproduced in the autobiographies of working men recounting their political, educational, or ethical transformation. The Temperance movement made the public signing of the pledge by new converts the centerpiece of their meetings. Similarly, the discourse of self-improvement, canonically articulated by Samuel Smiles's *Self-Help: With Illustrations of Character and Conduct* (1859), equated the cultivation of good character with its social performance so that it could be made legible to strangers.[52] During the second half of the nineteenth century, even the work of mesmerism, spiritualism, and occultism in exploring the deepest recesses of the self and the limits of its autonomy and rationality provided alternative, "scientific" stages for its realization and performance.[53] The modern social condition may have created a society of anonymous and distant strangers, but it also engendered new forms of intimacy, affection, and self-knowledge that ensured the personal relations remained at center of social life.

· · ·

Between 1750 and 1900, the rapid expansion, increasing mobility, and urban form of the British population created a new society of strangers. This new social condition—that I am suggesting is the condition of modernity—reshaped social relations on the streets, in our families, and in our interior worlds. It also demanded the development of new systems of government as well as new forms of association and exchange. It required literally reimagining and assembling a modern polity and economy.

CHAPTER THREE

Governing Strangers

Historians of Britain have now discovered so-called revolutions in government in every century since the Tudors.[1] Yet they all pale in comparison to that which had produced the modern state by the middle of the nineteenth century. As Weber recognized, this process depended upon the abstraction of the state's authority away from the figure of the monarch and his or her court, or the claims of particular politicians and local office holders, into faceless, bureaucratic systems. Gradually authority was relocated in new forms of disinterested expertise and administrative systems capable of addressing all subjects over distance in anonymous and uniform ways. Critical here, as Foucault taught us, was the capacity of these systems to map the population and territories over which its power extended and on whose security its claim to legitimacy rested. As place became space, people became populations, we moderns were conceived as objects of government in ways that meant we would never meet or know those who governed us.

This process was not unique to Britain. Yet although many of the techniques of bureaucratic abstraction were developed earlier and elsewhere, they were often driven by different impulses or worked on a different scale. Thus the civil service examinations in China, which dated back to the seventh century, worked not to impose an abstract bureaucracy upon an expanding imperial population but to train and discipline the administrators who would personify state power in their localities.[2] During the European Enlightenment, many forms of governmental abstraction were deployed and developed by reforming absolute monarchs and the revolutionary republics of America and France. Yet although these sometimes anticipated and sometimes preceded those in Britain, they were driven by political imperatives to extend the reach of government, the capacities of the state, and to refashion the forms of its legitimacy. This was also the case in Britain. New techniques of rule and the systemization of government made it possible to forge a new nation-state between the Acts of Union with Scotland and Ireland in 1707 and 1801 and to forge a new imperial polity that was capable of governing over hugely dispersed populations across several continents after the Seven Years War. Indeed, as we shall see, many of the new techniques of rule were developed to govern colonies.[3] Nonetheless, in Britain, these political imperatives were exaggerated by the problem of governing a rapidly growing and increasingly mobile population. In these conditions, the nature of power and authority, traditionally mediated through local and personal relations, had to be reinvented. The personal knowledge of, or charismatic authority over, a subject was no longer sufficient either in a highly mobile society of strangers or in an expanding imperial polity.

As ever in Britain, the forging of a modern and impersonal state was a gradual and accretive process. New systems and jurisdictions were layered on top of, and did not replace, older ones. By 1835 a single locality could come under the multiple jurisdictions of the parochial church vestry, the manorial court leet, justices of the peace, the county quarter sessions, the town council, and the poor law union. Yet rather than simply representing the survival of ancient forms of government, the increasingly variegated nature of the state at the local level highlights the dialectic in which the centralization and abstraction of state power generated fresh attempts to reembed it in new local and personal forms. Thus the transformation of Whitehall into a faceless government machine was offset by its reinvention as a ceremonial space, the revalorization of local forms of government and the personification of new state agencies in figures like the poor law guardian or the school attendance officer. By the mid-Victorian period the imperial British state was a different type of Leviathan from its precursors. Its ability to do more things over ever-greater distances was made possible by a new modus operandi of abstracted, standardized, and transferable systems of bureaucratic authority that nonetheless often continued to rest upon decidedly personal forms of power and authority.

THE GOVERNMENT MACHINE

Counting people, usually in order to raise taxes or armies, has been part of statecraft since the ancient world. Yet, during the eighteenth century, as a new spirit of quantification combined with a growing appetite of governments for knowledge of those populations they claimed sovereignty over, these exercises became more frequent and more accurate. In Britain this spirit of quantification was catalyzed during the late seventeenth century by new cultures of scientific experimentation interested in objectively measuring and reproducing results, the emergence of insurance as a business needing to quantify risks, and the use of "political arithmetick" to numerically demonstrate the efficiency and contribution of government to the wealth and health of the nation. Yet for all the ambition and occasional forays into the gathering of statistics and information on its subjects by the early modern state, it remained often localized and unsystematically organized.[4] Despite a false dawn in 1753, it was the double threat posed by war with revolutionary France and Malthus's warning of the inevitability of famine given the unprecedented scale of population growth that finally led Britain to conduct a census in 1801, following those by America and France a decade earlier.

The novelty of this census lay in its regularity (it was to be repeated every ten years), its simultaneity (it was conducted on a single day: March 10), the amount of information it collected (the address, number, sex, and occupations of household members, as well as dates of baptisms, marriages, and deaths from parish registers), the manner of its collection (with local parochial enumerators directed and supervised by district supervisors who in turn reported to a central office), and the forms of analysis and comparison it enabled (i.e., not just the size of the population as a whole but its location, occupation—in the three categories of trade, agriculture, or manufacturing—and family size, as well as its change over time in these categories). Never before had the state possessed such detailed knowledge of its population, even if it was confined to household data that were returned in aggregate form. Nonetheless, an official in London could now tell how many men and women lived in a particular village hundreds of miles away without leaving his office. Yet this was hardly a disembodied government machine at work. Until 1841 the parish officers of the Anglican Church collected the data because it was hoped they would possess personal knowledge of the households they had to inspect.

All that changed after the creation of the General Registrar Office (GRO) in 1836 (Scotland's came in 1855 and Ireland's in 1863). From the following year all births, deaths, and marriages were supposed to be returned to the state and not just the Anglican Church, although it was not compulsory to do so until 1875. Finally non-Anglican lives mattered and were legally recorded—previously they had rarely made the Anglican parish returns. England and Wales were divided into 626 registration districts with poor law commissioners appointed as registrars responsible for completing the quarterly register books and returning them to a regional superintendant registrar to check before forwarding to the GRO for another round of verification. In the first year alone there were a little under a million entries contained in twelve volumes stored in fireproof iron boxes. Even in a decade when statistical societies were being established in every major city, and other government departments were gathering and analyzing increasing quantities of statistics on crime, trade, poverty, education, and the size of the electorate, the GRO was a massive and innovative enterprise.[5]

When the GRO took over responsibility for the operation of the 1841 census, the population was individuated, that is, the names and details of each household member now had to be returned by enumerators. Thirty-five thousand local enumerators were appointed to oversee the completion of standardized forms that they had earlier delivered to households and whose returned information they had to enter in to special books. Once these books had been returned to the registrar general, officials abstracted the information so that it was possible to organize it in a variety of ways (e.g., by sex or occupation) or to analyze change over time (such as mobility or age). This work of analysis was exemplified by William Farr's discovery in 1851 that occupations like mining had very high rates of mortality. By statistically connecting the lives of geographically dispersed miners whose deaths could only previously be explained by local factors or the conditions of specific mines, he identified national patterns and trends that could inform the business of government. The collection and analysis of these statistics helped produce a different type of state with the capacity to think and act in new ways.

Censuses were introduced in Ireland and India soon after the imposition of colonial rule so the imperial state could know whom it governed. Twenty years after the Act of Union and the first census in England, Scotland, and Wales, the "United Kingdom" census was extended to Ireland. Census taking in India began eight years after the Revolt of 1857 when direct colonial rule replaced government through the East India Company. By 1881 it had become a massive decennial endeavor with half a million people serving as enumerators to collect the name, age, sex, occupation, residence, place of birth, caste, and religion of every person in India. It catalyzed a series of extensive analyses and reports that by the time of the 1901 census spread over a remarkable 60 volumes and embraced 295 million people with 147 different dialects and languages.[6] Yet despite the scale of these endeavors a *total*, abstract knowledge of colonial populations was never achieved. There were several reasons for this: the recalcitrance of those fearful of how the state would use the information; local enumerators not following guidelines and completing their forms from memory or personal knowledge rather than visits to households; the inability to easily categorize individuals as members of specific groups (whether as residents of a discernible address, or members of a particular race or religion).[7] Although censuses could be as much about the production of ignorance as knowledge, they had powerful consequences in the world. In India, caste categories were codified by the census and then entrenched within indigenous society as a basis for making claims against, or advancing interests within, the state.[8] Ignorance was then as productive of rule as knowledge. It did not matter that the state did not know what it got wrong; it mattered that it thought it had got it right and knew the strangers it sought to govern.

It was with the hope that all the subjects of the British Empire could be imagined as part of a single polity that the imperial census was finally conducted in 1901. Achieved with Joseph Chamberlain as colonial secretary, it was very much part of the various calls for imperial federation and cooperation that proliferated in the early twentieth century. In practice it was seemingly impossible to conceive of the empire as a single statistical unit. In 1901 whole populations or territories were excluded depending on the enthusiasm, diligence, and resources of colonial officials. Even in 1921, when the census recorded a staggering 458 million people spread across 13 million square miles, the only shared units of measurement was a basic head count and categorization by sex. The *Journal of the Royal Statistical Society* even ridiculed the accuracy of this data, noting that in parts of West Africa enumerators depended on the "casting of variously coloured beans into different pipkins by the head of each household, in order to denote the age and sex of those over whom he rules, or to the equally primitive count by knots tied in strings of different colours for each sex."[9] Local conditions always trumped the application of universal standards, and the imperial census of 1931 effectively proved the last. Marking the ambition to think of the empire as a single unit of government, in effect the imperial census served to demonstrate the dispersed and decentralized nature of colonial rule.[10]

Britain's newly inquisitive modern state may have had a voracious appetite for knowledge of the populations it sought to govern, but it shared much of that information with its subjects so that they could comprehend the rhythms of their collective life however distant and estranged they were. Farr's reports and analyses at the GRO may have been dry as dust, but they were feverishly engaged by the members of statistical societies that had proliferated since the 1830s, as well as by a far broader newspaper reading public. The Public Record Office (now called the National Archives) was created in 1838 to provide an archive for all this new data. Nonetheless, the number of those searching the public records remained remarkably small and dominated by those working for solicitor offices: by 1895 the total number of searches in the Public Record Office was under fifty-four thousand. In contrast, 645,000 people conduct nearly 3.5 million searches of the 1911 Census when the National Archives made it available online in January 2009.[11]

Just as the census allowed the state to know and govern its population abstractly, so the Ordinance Survey allowed it to know and map the territories of government. Here again war and the security of the state were critical. Although, under the threat of wartime invasion, southern coastal regions were mapped in 1791, by the time the Great Trigonometric Survey of India began in 1817 there were only maps for a third of England and Wales—the rest were not completed until 1853. The Ordinance Surveys of Ireland and Scotland had begun in 1824 and 1843 and were concluded in 1846 and 1882, respectively. They were huge operations. At its end the survey of Ireland employed two thousand people while the Indian survey necessitated a chain of triangulation that stretched fourteen hundred miles from its first baseline in Madras to the Himalayas (where fifty-foot towers had to be constructed to establish the apex of triangles). If the census's categories of enumeration shaped the way in which populations were understood, so the Ordinance Survey slowly assumed powers to collect, codify, and fix place names (often, of course, in standardized English), as well as determine administrative and property boundaries. These maps displaced a personal experience of place by a new uniform understanding of abstract space, subordinating customary local knowledge on the ground to that enabled from the bird's-eye view of the state. Indeed, the view of abstract space promoted by their clean geometric lines made unclaimed rural land and the irregular shapes of urban slums appear "unnatural." So detailed and effective had these methods become by the end of the nineteenth century that it took just a decade to plot Egypt on a scale of twenty-five inches to a mile in a series of twenty thousand maps that included the name of every landowner however small his plot. By the outbreak of World War I most of the vast territories of the British Empire had been mapped in these ways. Indeed, the strength of the state was itself projected not just in its access to detailed knowledge of far-flung localities but in the maps of the world, with Britain at its center and its extensive empire tinted a striking pink.[12]

Nowhere was the creation of a new type of faceless and bureaucratic modern state more apparent than in the reinvention of the practice of taxation. In early modern England, taxation was notoriously difficult to extract and collect. There was never enough tax revenue to fund the military ambitions of a Tudor and Stuart state that always labored under the fear that more or different forms of taxation would provoke rebellion. Yet a new type of fiscal-military state emerged from the late seventeenth century. Its novelty rested in the creation of a new financial instrument—the national debt—that allowed the state to borrow enough money through the newly formed Bank of England (1694) to fund its military ambitions. Reliable streams of tax revenue were necessary to secure these loans and to service them at lower rates of interest. These came from three sources. Nearly half came from a land tax and the rest from a combination of custom and excise duties. Both the land tax and custom duties were collected directly from landowners and merchants by laymen acting as agents of the state. But the excise duties (the equivalent of contemporary sales tax targeted on particular commodities) established a whole new system of tax collection that was so effective it accounted for a growing proportion of government revenue, rising from 29 percent in 1710 to 80 percent by 1820.[13]

The Board of Excise developed an administrative system of unprecedented scale and sophistication in three ways. Firstly, it divided the country into 886 "districts" and assigned each of its growing number of excise men (more than 2,000 by 1708) a particular set of daily circuits that consisted on average of thirty-eight-mile rural "rides" and six-mile urban "walks." Widely known and recognized on their circuits, excisemen, like the agents responsible for collecting land tax and customs, developed personal relations with those they were responsible for taxing, so that assessment and verification sometimes depended on oaths, honor, and trust. Secondly, to temper the local varieties such practices generated, each excise man was armed with a technical apparatus of manuals, gauges, and measures to provide uniform and transferable standards of assessment across the country. Increasingly the authority and reliability of the excise man depended upon new bureaucratic systems like standardized weights and measures (especially after the introduction of the new imperial system in 1824) and double-entry book-keeping that became compulsory after the abolition of oath taking in the 1840s. The message, as one historian has put it, was clear: "Don't trust us but trust in our procedures and instruments".[14] Thirdly, rationalization and standardization of duties reduced their number from the 1,500 different rates operating in 1800 to twenty-six general categories by 1860. By the end of the nineteenth century a mere nine commodities were subject to excise duties, and just four of those (foreign spirits, tobacco, tea, and wine) generated 96 percent of total excise revenue. The creation of a seemingly disinterested bureaucratic system—predicated upon standardized forms of measurement, assessment, and collection—became the hallmarks of the modern system of taxation that became normalized during the nineteenth century.

This system found its apogee with the introduction of income tax. First introduced to help fund the Napoleonic Wars between 1799 and

1815, income tax was permanently reinstated in 1842 and signaled a slow shift away from the state's dependence on indirect forms of taxation. If excise tax had fueled the state's military ambitions during the eighteenth century, so income tax helped fund the extension of the state's civil capacities and infrastructures during the nineteenth century. And yet unlike all previous forms of taxation, it was almost from inception a faceless procedure, abstracted to a set of forms and procedures—notably the use of taxation schedules—that allowed deduction at source. By 1870 the entire system was operated by just 361 surveyors and inspectors who remained anonymous to the taxpayer. There remained important exceptions here, because profits from land (as well as trade, commerce, and professional activities) continued to be negotiated and collected in person by a network of fifty-four thousand local lay assessors and commissioners, usually of a professional class status. With incomes that had to exceed £100 a year, and with a relatively small rate of remuneration of 1.5 pennies per pound (a pound consisted then of 240 pennies) of tax collected, these lay officials were expected to be disinterested, discrete, and not too inquisitorial of those they assessed. Unsurprisingly, the Inland Revenue feared that this system encouraged underevaluation, and although attempts were made to remove the lay element in 1864, it was not until the 1920s that the Revenue finally gained control of local assessment and collection. Only then did the assessment and collection of taxation become naturalized around an entirely faceless, bureaucratic process.[15]

Taxation was no less central to colonial state formation. As always India provided an important testing ground of new systems that illustrated the rule of difference. With pressure from London to increase its revenues and to eradicate the corruption of tax collectors who amassed personal fortunes, the East India Company under Cornwallis introduced an ambitious Permanent Settlement of tax demands upon landholders in Bengal during 1793. At the heart of the system was a new fixed rate of tax upon land which was levied upon landholding *zamindars,* who, in return, were provided with security of tenure and effective ownership of peasant plots as long as they paid their allotted taxes. Although it represented an attempt, still unimaginable in Britain, to create a universal standard and subject of taxation, it was also a system intended to discipline the company's district officers who served as collectors. The dependence upon the personal skills and knowledge of district officers was no less evident when income tax was introduced in 1886 to service the growing expenditure of the colonial state after the Revolt of 1857. Ostensibly modeled on the "fairness" of the British system of schedules, universal standards of assessment, and anonymous forms of collection, it boasted few of these things. As payment at source was made compulsory only for public employees, more than half of the total tax revenue was collected by officers who had to assess who was liable to taxation (including private companies and partnerships) and then calculate their liability without a uniform standard for either declaring income or assessing it. Unsurprisingly, taxation remained a matter of reputation and negotiation, with a third of taxpayers appealing to the district officer, who, in the company of his assessors, wielded considerable personal authority.[16]

Yet it was standardized and anonymous bureaucratic systems that allowed Britain's imperial state to massively extend its knowledge of its subjects during the twentieth century. The introduction of national insurance in 1911 required a continuous and complete knowledge of the employment history and income of the 2 million men whose loss of earnings through ill health or redundancy it protected after fifteen weeks. When national insurance was extended to the entire adult population in 1946, its labor of documentation demanded the attention of about four thousand staff at the Ministry of Pensions. As with the Inland Revenue, it was only those considered delinquent—those evading tax or "farming" benefits—who encountered the human face of this otherwise faceless government machine. If these inspectors personified the power of the state—and sometimes appeared to enjoy the experience—their knowledge of those they inspected was bureaucratic, not personal: it came from an intimate knowledge of their files, not their lives.[17]

The abstraction of state power through anonymous administrative systems required a new machinery of government. The inquisitive state depended upon the technical means of gathering and processing vast quantities of data, and this involved a complex assemblage of standardized forms, trained personnel, and machines. The training of enumerators, registrars, and inspectors relied not just on their manuals but the standardized forms they had to complete to ensure that comparable and consistent data were gathered regardless of where they were collected or by whom. Once collected locally, this data had to be aggregated and processed from the center. The techniques for doing this developed over time in synch with the quantity and complexity of data: the mid-nineteenth century was the era of the ledger, the late nineteenth and early twentieth centuries the era of the card index file, the mid-twentieth century the Hollerith machine, and then, finally, the computer. What the state did and how it was able to bring all its subjects, regardless of distance, within a single frame of analysis and action depended upon these techniques and machines.[18] They were constitutive of the state, not simply a product of its increasingly inquisitive ambitions.

Human capital was no less important to the representation of the government machine as disinterested and scientific. The Northcote-Trevelyan Report of 1854, which invented the term *civil service* adeptly promoted this view. It represented the administrative classes of the seventeenth and eighteenth centuries as corrupt and inefficient: offices were sold or delivered by ministers or patrons, appointments made for the duration of "the kings pleasure", and venal practices allowed officials to supplement their incomes. In contrast, the report argued, the neutrality and efficiency of the civil service could be achieved only when office holders were anonymous to the public, and permanent appointments (supported by adequate salaries and pensions) were made through open competitions. In fact, the Northcote-Trevelyan Report was closer to the end than the beginning of a process of reform and rationalization. A product of the East India Company's administrative class, Trevelyan was recruited through old patronage networks but trained at the colleges of Haileybury and Fort William and subjected to exams that streamed the company's officers into different classes and positions of service. He was also the brother-in-law of Thomas Macaulay, who had pushed through further reforms of the civil service in India during the 1830s. Indeed, two years before the publication of the Northcote-Trevelyan Report, entrance to the civil service in India was opened up by a competitive exam, albeit one held in London and thus excluding virtually all Indians![19] It was not until the 1880s that Whitehall's new Civil Service Commission enforced new professional standards—demarcating departmental responsibilities and the duties of each appointment, calibrating salaries to the complexity of work, and creating a division of labor between an elite group of administrative generalists presiding over the more routine and mechanical work of clerks and those with specialist knowledge.[20] By the late nineteenth century the civil service in both India and Britain had successfully made disinterested service an ethos and bureaucratic process a vocation.

Although Queen Victoria was reportedly horrified that the administrative reforms heralded by the Northcote-Trevelyan Report would create a new breed of independent and faceless bureaucrats, it actually produced a new governing caste. This caste styled themselves as gentlemen and cultivated very particular understandings of the personal character and social milieu of the administrator. Upper-division clerks were considered generalists capable of careful analysis and considered judgment, and their disinterested style of thought and independence of character was identified as the preserve of a gentlemanly liberal arts education at certain private schools and Oxbridge.[21] There were 450 members of this elite group in 1914, and 78 percent of them were Oxbridge graduates, where a remarkable 60 percent had read Classics. Because an Oxbridge education was not available to nonconformists or women until the 1870s, the clerks were almost universally male and Anglican. Men of this gentlemanly caliber, especially when fortified by good salaries and pensions, were considered safe guardians of the state's secrets. Arguably it was not until the late twentieth century, when the professional qualities of this caste were finally separated from a specific social class, that the civil service finally became "open." Even by 1969, when there were 1,089 civil servants in the highest administrative class, only 5 percent were women, 64 percent went to Oxbridge, and 96 percent were educated privately or in selective grammar schools.[22]

Below this elite caste of gentlemanly governors came the so-called specialists, men with specific technical knowledge upon which the state's expanding services depended. These men were not the products of the character factories of private schools and Oxbridge; their expertise lay instead in a particular body of scientific or technical knowledge—they were engineers, surveyors, statisticians, actuaries, veterinarians, chemists, medics, meteorologists, and so on. Although not an invention of the 1830s, their numbers grew significantly over the following decades when they were joined by increasing numbers of inspectors. As the mobile eyes and ears of government, the inspectors spread out across the country to regulate the conditions of mines, factories, prisons, workhouses, and schools, as well as the very broadly defined nuisances (later termed "sanitary conditions"), which included the regulation of lodging and slaughter houses, highways, house-to-house inspections, as well as the regulation of food, air, and water quality. Although their disinterested authority came from their professional expertise, inspectors were far from faceless bureaucrats. Theoretically the inspector was a technician whose task was to record and measure things armed with a panoply of portable instruments and centrally determined scientific standards. Yet because their work required continual interaction with the public, the personal arts of discretion and diplomacy were indispensable. In remote areas like the Isle of Skye, where in 1895 a single individual was responsible for all forms of inspection and walked almost three thousand miles completing his duties, it was especially difficult to separate the bureaucratic process from the arts of personal relations.[23]

Lastly, in the carefully constructed hierarchy of the civil service, came the lower-division clerks tasked with the so-called mechanical work of copying and drafting that was so important to the flow of information through government departments. By 1871 there were two thousand of these workers paid a uniform rate of 10 pence an hour, and by 1875 they were supplemented by a new category of "boy" clerk who was routinely released at age twenty. The increasing speed and quantity of correspondence required a veritable army of scribes with no knowledge or training bar a good and swift hand. Because this group lacked the generous salary, career structure, and social prestige of the higher classes, they were assumed to lack the gentlemanly discretion required to maintain the secrecy of state information in the face of an increasingly predatory press. In 1911 the culture of honorable secrecy, which had been so central to the ethos of the reformed civil service, was supplemented with an Official Secrets Act designed to ensure that not even the low-caste clerks would dare to leak information.[24]

If this new machinery of government was never entirely impersonal, neither was it ever simply abstract. It was materialized in the shape of roads, rails, ships and aircraft, telegraph cables, and radio transmitting stations that allowed the state to extend and make manifest the reach of its power. Although this communications infrastructure eased the business of government by allowing for the increasingly speedy transmission of data over ever-greater distances, it was invariably a product of military imperatives that ensured that the violent force of the state was very much apparent. Just as Britain's interkingdom roads were laid after the unions with Scotland and Ireland, so soldiers, whose barracks were strategically positioned by trunk roads, marched around the country on rotation, and were frequently deployed to quell riots and disorders. Twelve thousand marched to London during the Gordon Riots of 1780, and the same number was sent to "pacify" the Luddite disturbances between Leicester and York in 1811 and 1812. Soon troops were deployed by rail, most famously when eight thousand troops were sent to London to enforce a ban on the planned Chartist procession to Parliament in 1848. By road or rail, the mobility of troops was essential given the nascent and inadequate nature of the new police forces created in the 1820s and 1830s. With the exception of London, where the Metropolitan Police grew steadily and answered directly to the Home Office, many towns and cities were remarkably slow in developing police forces. In 1848, 13 percent of incorporated boroughs in England and Wales still lacked police forces, as did 41.5 percent of rural counties five years later. Where police forces did exist, their officers were so thin on the ground that they were incapable of controlling serious disturbances without reading the Riot Act and calling for the military. In 1841 there was but just one police officer for every nine hundred inhabitants in London and around six hundred for Manchester and Birmingham—and these compared favorably to more than 1,000 for Leeds, 2,200 for Walsall, 3,200 for Macclesfield. Even though the police force grew considerably in the second half of the nineteenth century—by 1881 there were only 32,000 for a population of 26 million in England and Wales, an average of one policeman for every 812 inhabitants—it remained a largely symbolic presence in many towns and cities.[25] Even by the early twentieth century, as with the Great Transport Strike of 1911 or the General Strike of 1926, it was still necessary to deploy troops to quell unrest. If the violent force of the nation-state had a human face, it was that of a stranger.

Moving troops around Britain was considerably easier than sustaining armies abroad. Given the logistical problems of supplying a distant army during the eighteenth century, overseas land wars were fought by dint of local alliances and hired hands. Thus the Battle of Plassey in 1757, when Britain was also fighting in Europe and North America, was won with just 750 British soldiers and some 2,000 Indian Sepoys. Up to the 1760s some 25 percent of expenditure on the Army went to hiring foreign troops. Nonetheless, with improved chains of supply the British Army grew almost tenfold between 1689 and 1815, when it reached 400,000. The Navy was critical to the deployment and support of the Army across the empire. By the late nineteenth century it accounted for a fifth of all government expenditure. Policing the distant lands of the empire catalyzed increasing the size, speed, and power of the fleet. It was the use of iron-hulled gunboats to patrol the Ganges, Tigris, and

Euphrates, as well as China's port towns during the Opium Wars, that finally persuaded the Navy to abandon wooden ships.

Although increasingly effective systems of transportation allowed the state to reach further and faster afield than before, so new technologies allowed it to wield its violent force at an increasing distance. Technologically this was a nineteenth-century development, for as Daniel Headrick suggests, "the disparity between the rifle of World War One and the Napoleonic musket was greater than between the musket and the bow and arrow."[26] Muskets had an accurate range of between fifty and seventy yards at the end of the eighteenth century, but a variety of technical improvements in barrel and bullet design had increased this to close to three hundred yards by the mid-nineteenth century. The introduction of the breech-loading, bolt-action rifle from the 1860s increased the ranges to five hundred yards and allowed for quicker reloading. With the introduction of Gatling machine guns in the colonial wars against Zulus and Ashanti in southern Africa during the 1870s, as well as in Egypt the following decade, reloading became unnecessary. As new techniques of indirect firing began to replace the direct line of sight to the target, the uses of artillery weapons were also transformed from the 1870s. And finally came airplanes and aerial bombardment. In 1919 alone aerial attacks were used to quell unrest in Egypt, India, Afghanistan, and Somaliland, and they were soon deployed to equally devastating effect in Iraq, Palestine, Sudan, and Ireland. It was, however, in Iraq during the 1920s that Arthur "Bomber" Harris appears to have gained his first experience with the system of blanket bombing he would unleash upon Dresden and Hamburg during the Second World War. Needless to say, precision—let alone the distinction between the civilian and military target—was less important than the moral effect of mass and impersonal destruction by a state that had a seemingly omnipotent power to let live or let die. Killing was now industrial in scale and impersonal in nature. Hand-to-hand combat had not been eradicated, but killing another human being had certainly become a more abstract prospect even if the drone strike was still some way off.

Unleashing the violent force of the state over distance relied in part on a communications system able to quickly identify where it was required. The successive development of post, telegraph, and radio dramatically compressed the space and time of government. The state had operated a postal system since the seventeenth century along the roads to Bristol, Hollyhead, Dover, Edinburgh, Norwich, and Plymouth. With the introduction of mail coaches on roads in 1784 and by rail from 1838, the network considerably extended while retaining London as its hub. The mail was the way the central state communicated with its local officers. Until the introduction of the Penny Post in 1840, a franking system ensured that members of Parliament and officials could use the system for free. Seven million letters were circulated in this way in 1838, and unlike the 57 million regular letters sent that year (which were charged by distance), they were evenly spread across the country. Creating a postal system was one of the first requirements of colonial government. The first postal system in Ireland had been established in the 1640s to facilitate communication between London and its rebellious colony. The East India Company established a postal system within its three presidencies during the 1760s, but it was in 1854 that a centralized postal system was introduced in India around prepaid stamps and delivery via rail. The Irish post was incorporated within the British system in the 1830s, and its equation with colonial power was made evident when the Dublin Post Office was seized in the Easter Rising of 1916.[27]

In 1845 the Post Office also became the home of a telegraph system that allowed signals to be sent and received over enormous distances almost simultaneously. By 1870 the telegraph network in Britain alone included twenty-two thousand miles of cable and generated 6 million messages from over three thousand points. By 1852 a cable had crossed the Irish Sea, and by 1865 there were reliable cables running across the Atlantic to North America as well as the Red Sea to India. Thereafter the tentacles of cables spread across the empire to Hong Kong (1871), New Zealand (1876), and eastern and southern Africa (1879). Whereas in the 1860s and 1870s short messages could take days to arrive, by the end of the century transmission took barely half an hour. No other system of communication became so vital to the business of colonial administration in times of crises. The telegraph had first facilitated troop movements in Britain during the Chartist agitation, but it was during the Revolt in India that it became indispensable, with 4,500 miles of cable facilitating rapid deployments when correspondence with London still took weeks.[28] If the telegraph substantially eased the business of governing over distance, it also created a new temporal coherence to the territories of the state. Simultaneity in telegraphic transmission along railway lines allowed for the standardization of national and eventual global time. This process began in Britain during the 1840s, when rail companies started publishing timetables of arrivals and departures that were synchronized around London rather than locally managed time. By the 1850s most cities were reconciling themselves to the new time discipline emanating from London, but it was a different story in more remote rural areas where trains and telegraphs rarely reached until the Definition of Time Act of 1880 legislated a standardized national time. The same process occurred across the empire and indeed the world as rails and cables spread across it, and by 1884 the world centered its time grid on London's Greenwich Mean Time.

THE CHARISMATIC STATE

Governing a society of strangers and an expanding imperial polity may have produced a new machinery of government with increasingly abstract and impersonal forms of rule, but these in turn often generated the creation of equally novel charismatic and highly personalized forms of power. This dialectic was apparent to the journalist Walter Bagehot in 1867 when he outlined how *The English Constitution* revolved around not just what he characterized as its "efficient" parts that got the business of government done but the almost mystical aura that surrounded its "dignified" parts like the monarchy.[29] The point for Bagehot, and for me, is that both were not just necessary, they worked together. Thus the growing ranks of the new civil service in Whitehall and their bureaucratic equipment ensured that the state took a monumental material form. During the nineteenth century the area between Trafalgar and Parliament squares, as well as the new Victoria Embankment, became *the* bureaucratic space of government. Once the site of the royal court, which is why the Houses of Parliament were originally built there in the fifteenth century, much of Whitehall and its many private mansions were destroyed by fire in 1698. Even though the fiscal-military state stamped its presence upon the space during the eighteenth century— rebuilding the Admiralty Office (1726) and then constructing the Treasury (1736) and the Board of Trade (1768)—the modern character of Whitehall was forged with the reconstruction of the Houses of Parliament (1840–60) after the fire of 1834, the redesign of Trafalgar Square around the new National Gallery (1832–38) and Nelson's Column (1845), as well as the hotly debated design for the new Foreign and India Offices (1868–73).[30] Just as important, the space itself was then opened up by the creation of the Victoria Embankment (1870) and the widening of Parliament Street by the removal of King's Street at the entrance to Parliament Square (1873) (see figure 10). Downing Street became the official residence and office of the prime minister and chancellor of the exchequer in 1885, and a series of new monumental ministries of state were built: the Home and Colonial Offices (1873–75), New Scotland Yard (1888–91 and 1912), the Admiralty extensions (1895 and 1911 with Admiralty Arch), the Treasury (1898–1917), and the War Office (1899–1906). The historicist styles of these buildings belied the novelty of their construction and announced the permanence and solidity of the state. Yet behind these façades lay deeply functional spaces designed to allow the armies of clerks to get the business of government done: the new War Office had more than a thousand offices and two and a half miles of corridors.[31]

In its new monumental form, Whitehall became reenchanted as the ceremonial center of the imperial state. Fittingly for the site of the old

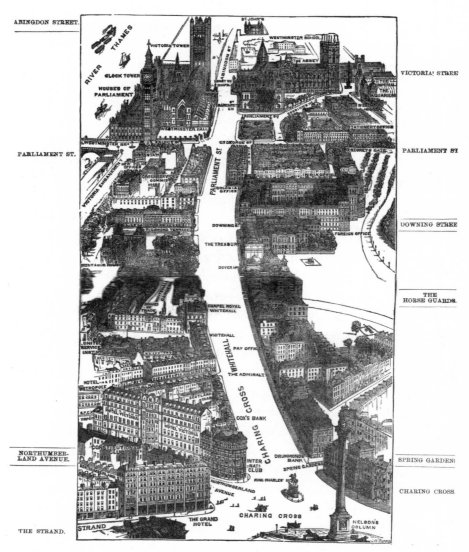

Figure 10. The "Dignified" Space of Whitehall. Labels for "Whitehall Gardens," "The Horse Guards," and "The Parade" have been omitted from the middle of the image, from left to right.

Source: Herbert Fry, *London* (London: W. H. Allen, 1891).

royal court, Whitehall became the stage for a reinvented monarchy to perform. Slowly denuded of its executive power during the nineteenth century, the monarchy was increasingly invested with renewed symbolic currency. Queen Victoria began the ritualized state opening of Parliament in 1852, but following the death of her husband only did so six times between 1861 and 1886, even after Disraeli had made her Empress of India in 1877. It was Edward VII who cemented the place and lavish style of the state opening of Parliament, just as he carved out the monarchy's own distinctive space in Whitehall by building Admiralty Arch, widening the Mall, and refinishing the façade of Buckingham Palace in the decade before the Great War. As the imperial state's ceremonial and bureaucratic heart, Whitehall became the target of Fenian bombs in 1883 and 1885; the suffragettes protested there two decades later by chaining themselves to railings or smashing the windows of government offices. Whitehall was the obvious site for the Allied Victory Parade in 1919 and the cenotaph constructed at its center for the annual ceremony to remember the veterans of the Great War. The architect of that cenotaph, Edwin Lutyens, was busily engaged in designing British India's new and very expensive capital city of New Delhi (1912–31) as the challenges to British rule were mounting and its permanence appeared less than cast in stone. Lutyens's work is a poignant reminder that the monumental architecture, which spread across the empire from the 1870s, promoted a distinctly imperial vision of the British state with Whitehall at its center.[32]

As the spectacular scale of the Secretariat buildings in New Delhi demonstrated, nowhere was the bureaucratic abstraction of colonial government more evident than in India. Yet governing at a distance across the British Empire was also made possible by other means. When the reins of colonial government tightened in India after the Revolt of 1857, it was accompanied with the growth of ceremonial spectacles and charismatic forms of personal rule. The imperial reinvention of the Durbar to mark Queen Victoria's coronation as Empress of India in 1877 paled in comparison to the show put on by Lord Curzon in 1903 to celebrate the coronation of King Edward VII. Furthermore, although the East India Company had long depended upon its alliances with hundreds of princely rulers who governed almost a third of India's territory, their position was secured after the imposition of direct rule in 1858, when, in return for their loyalty and support of the Indian Army, they were excused from taxation. Although advised by members of the Indian Civil Service, princely rulers were left to rule in highly personal ways as autocrats for good or ill. Even those who promoted administrative reforms, representative assemblies, sanitary and educational infrastructures invariably did so as an extension of their personal authority.[33]

Indirect rule and the personification of the imperial state were not confined to India. In Cape Colony the British afforded Xhosa chiefs authority over their own customary affairs but sought to impose the power of the imperial state through the personal authority of the governor. The governor established that authority by touring the province with his retinue, summoning the chiefs to assembly meetings, and appointing resident agents or commissioners to each tribe to oversee the operation of Xhosa and British law (British law was imposed in cases of murder, witchcraft, and theft). These routines were not enough for Sir Harry Smith. When he became governor in 1847 he invented new charismatic displays of his authority such as insisting chiefs kiss his feet and claiming the Xhosa title of Great Chief *(Inkoshi Enkulu)* for himself.[34] As the British Empire expanded so dramatically in the final quarter of the nineteenth century its reliance on indirect forms of rule grew. From Malaya to Fiji, and across the continent of Africa, sultans, kings, sheikhs, and tribal chiefs were allowed to maintain their personal authority—and their peoples' cultural and religious traditions upon which it was deemed to rest—in return for following the advice of the British representative installed beside them as governors, resident generals, or commissioners. When Lord Lugard, the governor of Nigeria, famously celebrated this system of imperial rule in *The Dual Mandate* (1922), he effectively codified what had already been in operation in many colonies for more than a century. All that changed was the impressively gaudy scale with which the imperial state manufactured pomp, circumstance, and ceremony to enhance the personal authority of its governors and native rulers.[35]

The figure of the district officer nicely illustrates how the personification of power in the colonial context was never simply a replacement for the more expensive impersonal forms of bureaucratic government. A creation of the East India Company in British India, the district officer was chiefly responsible for collecting taxes and maintaining law and order in districts that could extend to four thousand square miles. In the bureaucratic hierarchy they were accountable to a commissioner, who in turn answered to the governor through his provincial secretaries, but in practice a good deal of autonomy was ceded to the district officer as the proverbial "man on the spot." This was hardly surprising given that even at its height the Indian Civil Service boasted little more than a thousand civil servants governing over 300 million Indians with a myriad of languages. The Colonial Service sought to reproduce the Indian model of the district officer in Africa. Trained as generalists in accounting, local economies and histories, criminal and Islamic law, hygiene and sanitation, surveying, ethnology, and language, district officers in Africa worked in remote conditions without much guidance. In 1906 there was one European civil servant to every 45,000 Nigerians, and even by 1914 there were just 252 district officers covering 372,674 miles of territory. Kenya was no different, with 120 district officers covering 224,960 square miles in 1909. They were expected to tour their districts "to show the flag," collect taxes, administer the law, perform ceremonial functions, and discern the mood of the population through village meetings, personal visits, and letters. Despite having to correspond with the provincial office and national secretariat, the district officer's work in Africa was hardly that of a faceless bureaucrat.[36]

These forms of local and personal rule were not confined to the remote edges of empire. As the reach of Whitehall's bureaucratic authority extended in Britain during the nineteenth century, so suspicion of it ensured that most legislation was adoptive and only implemented if localities chose to do so. When compulsion came it was invariably counterbalanced by the creation of new local structures and bodies. The New Poor Law of 1834 may have created a central Poor Law Commission and an army of inspectors to ensure that its directives were being followed, but locally elected poor law guardians administered poor relief. By 1860 only 60 percent of local unions had built the mandated new workhouses, and even during the 1890s 76 percent were still providing the outdoor relief the New Poor Law had been introduced to eradicate. Poor law guardians enjoyed considerable personal authority and often prided themselves on their intimate knowledge of the poor and local conditions. Local union elections became especially animated affairs after 1894, when the requirement to own property, or be a justice of the peace or magistrate to become a guardian was dropped and the system of plural voting (which gave more votes to the rich and none to women) was scrapped. Similarly, the creation of school boards for the local administration of compulsory state education in 1870—also overseen by a central board of education and an inspectorate—considerably enlivened politics at the local level. In many spheres, then, the growth of a centralized bureaucratic state reanimated local political structures.

Moreover, as state agencies proliferated, they were frequently afforded a human face on the ground. The imposition of compulsory education required school attendance officers with not just intimate knowledge of their neighborhoods but with powers of persuasion, the physical prowess to drag children to school, and the willingness to prosecute parents of those delinquent. As children became the objects of a growing number of state interventions in the early twentieth century, nearly all depended upon officials—like school medical officers, health visitors, and probation officers—whose jobs were to work in communities through face-to-face relationships with parents and their offspring. Like inspectors, these officials were charged with implementing new standards of care and discipline, but this was achieved by persuasion as much as by coercion, even if we know from their logbooks and memoirs that they administered as much contempt as empathy to those they encountered.[37] In many instances it was impossible to imagine the abstraction of the state behind its new bureaucratic authority without these figures providing it with a local and human face.

. . .

We can conclude, then, that from the eighteenth century new forms of bureaucratic organization, techniques of abstraction, and material infrastructures were developed that allowed power and authority to become impersonal and extend over greater distances in new ways. By the middle of the nineteenth century, these innovations produced a new and distinctly modern type of state capable of both governing over a society of strangers and forging an imperial polity with an unprecedented global reach. Although many of these new impersonal forms of bureaucratic government, like the very idea of a disinterested civil service, were first developed in India, the modern state was not simply a colonial invention. Much like the civil service exams that operated in China from the seventh century, the new bureaucratic forms of colonial government were frequently deployed to discipline administrators who were accustomed to lining their own pockets and introducing a good deal of personal power into following central standards and procedures. Which is not to say that bureaucratic and charismatic forms of authority were necessarily at odds, because they were often symbiotic. However large the new Leviathan of the modern state became, however far its machinery of government extended, its power was also made manifest and produced by equally new charismatic forms around buildings, ceremonies, and people.

CHAPTER FOUR

Associating with Strangers

A founding conceit of British history is the claim that Britain made the modern world by being the first to develop a system of representative politics and a civil society whose culture of public debate ensured that the Leviathan of the state remained tethered. It was a story told by Thomas Macaulay's last volume of *The History of England* in 1848 as revolutions wracked continental Europe, and still rehearsed (albeit less triumphantly) by Jürgen Habermas in the late twentieth century.[1] And it goes something like this: The stormy conflicts of the seventeenth century were followed by an Enlightened eighteenth-century dawn whose vibrant associational and intellectual life, facilitated by the growth of print culture, enabled the nineteenth century reform of an electoral system that allowed the opinions of individuals to triumph over influence and corruption. So representative did politics become that Britain was able to avoid revolution. This is a caricature for sure, but, despite all the subtle arguments about how and when this happened, it captures the essential flavor of a still somewhat self-congratulatory historiography. Nonetheless there are those who insist either that the persistence of aristocratic power meant the state was not rendered fully representative or that the new forms of civil society inscribed rules about how politics was organized, conducted, and understood which ensured citizens were no less free of government.[2]

This debate about whether Britain became more or less democratic (however we might understand that) does not seem a good way of assessing when its politics became modern. If we abandon those normative claims, it is possible to see more clearly how the structure of politics was fundamentally transformed as it faced the challenges posed by the increasing size, mobility, and anonymity of Britain's population and its extension overseas across the empire. The advent of a society of strangers and the extension of the imperial polity meant that no less than state power popular politics could no longer be organized around its familiar local and personal networks. Civil society was restructured upon new forms of abstraction. Print culture was vital in enabling strangers to imagine themselves as a community of sentiment that defied geography, but they were bound together and mobilized by new bureaucratic organizations. The act of voting was also transformed as electors became defined not by local traditions but uniform national standards and procedures that imagined all electors as anonymous individuals whose votes were no longer accountable to their communities. Local and personal forms of civil society were never entirely erased, and they were actively promoted by those distrustful of the increasingly abstract modes of conducting politics.

A CIVIL SOCIETY OF STRANGERS

Clearly, early modern civil society was not solely rooted in local networks and face-to-face encounters. London was only the most obvious exception. Yet, even there, coffee houses illustrated that associational life could remain remarkably intimate. As coffee houses flourished in the late seventeenth century they became hubs. They were places where friends and strangers alike met to exchange almost everything (gossip, news, ideas, commodities, bets, even professional services) and to form new businesses, clubs, and associations. By 1739 there were 551 of them in London. The fashionable periodical the *Spectator* (1711–14) was a product of this culture. The fictional character of its title wryly observed the associational life of the metropolis, playing on its readers' familiarity with particular places, persons, or types. As London's population grew, so did the number of its clubs and societies: around a thousand existed in 1750. In contrast, cities like Bristol, with fifty thousand inhabitants, had a dozen or so different types of associations, whereas places like Northampton, with a population of just five thousand, had only three.[3] Although the numbers of clubs and voluntary societies had risen suddenly in the first half of the eighteenth century, they grew exponentially in its second half. Although many of these were the product of distinct local or regional networks, the freemasons, moral reform societies and Methodism spread more widely as a consequence of the increased mobility of the population. New Masonic lodges were, for instance, established by traveling gentlemen to help cement personal relations with those they met and did business with. There were 180 lodges in Britain by 1740, and by 1800 they had spread across much of the empire in South Asia, North America, the Caribbean, West Africa, and the South Pacific. A century later there were no less than 737 imperial lodges (with 321 in India alone by 1930!). When freemasons declared that by an expanding circle of personal relations they had established "a vast chain extending round the whole globe," it was not mere bombast.[4] It was a model later replicated further down the social scale as Methodist preachers and apprentices on the tramp sought the comfort of strangers who were fellow believers or craftsmen. Local craftsmen frequently formed clubs to discuss mutual interests and forge personal as well as organizational ties between localities by accommodating those looking for work from elsewhere. Seventeen trades had developed these extralocal but interpersonal networks by 1800.[5] Yet despite some precocious national and imperial networks, Britain's associational culture was predominantly mediated by personal relations and local solidarities often cemented through the performance of oaths and ceremonies.

Extending beyond the local and regional required a formalized organizational structure, not just personal connections or relationships. Peter Clark has detected a shift from informally organized local clubs and societies to those that increasingly required national constitutions, subscriptions, journals, and even purpose-built meeting halls in the late eighteenth century.[6] Friendly societies, which by 1850 boasted 4 million members (half of the adult male population), are a good example. Spreading most rapidly in the new urban centers, they promoted forms of mutuality that made strangers have the obligations of friends. In the largest order, the Odd Fellows, it was long held that such obligations were best germinated locally through personal relations and ritualized performances. Opposition toward national federation was overcome partly by bureaucratic formalization. The Odd Fellows established their own journal with reports from local lodges to foster a sense of a national community; they disseminated printed copies of rules, toasts, and sermons and established a representative organizational structure around regional districts and an annual conference that moved every year. Yet this structure was engrafted on top of the continuing importance attached to local and personal relations, whether through the performance of rituals at local lodges or the visits of national leaders to them.[7]

In the early nineteenth century, trade unions were also increasingly organized into regional divisions with common rules, headquarters, and occasional meetings of local representatives. The repeal of the Combination Acts in 1824 allowed for the development of more effective national systems of communication and organization, complete with secretaries and elected officials as well as trade reports and journals. Nonetheless the localities remained responsible for the collection of subscriptions, the distribution of benefits, and calls for local action. The importance of locality was also apparent with the proliferation of local trades councils in the second half of the nineteenth century. Only from the 1850s did unions amalgamating across trades assume a genuinely national form. The Amalgamated Society of Engineers, founded in 1850, developed an impressive national organizational structure in

London that handled subscriptions, benefits, and representative decision making; by the 1860s, it had thirty thousand members across three hundred branches. This structure allowed those who had never met, let's say a machinist in Manchester and a patternmaker in Birmingham, understand their common interests as engineers and unite behind a campaign for national standards of pay and conditions.[8]

The spread and formalization of associational culture did not stop at the shores of the British Isles. Since the eighteenth century, British sports had spread across the empire with its emigrating population, but it was not until the 1860s and 1870s that the rules of the games were standardized by the creation of central organizations like the Football Association (1863), Rugby Football Union (1871), and Lawn Tennis Association (1888).[9] International competitions, rules, and governing bodies followed swiftly—sometimes overtly in competition with the British imperial standard. Thus, despite the English, Welsh, Scottish, and Irish Football Associations (FA) forming the International Football Association Board in 1886, its rival Fédération Internationale de Football Association (FIFA) was established in Paris in 1904.

This bureaucratic formalization of extra-local affinities was also evident in the culture of politics. Petitioning, for instance, had been around for centuries as a way by which local communities asked the monarch to redress their grievances or advance their interests. When petitions began to be printed in the 1650s, they extended beyond the locality or region and collected more signatures: thus between 1640 and 1660 a total of five hundred petitions collected an unprecedented twenty thousand signatures. By the 1680s, when they were increasingly addressed to Parliament (not the monarch) and used to invoke and influence publics beyond it, there were routinely two hundred petitions a year. A century later the campaign against the slave trade provided the peak of eighteenth-century petitioning, with 500 petitions collecting more than 350,000 signatures in the single year of 1792. Compare this to the height of petitioning between 1838 and 1842, when there was an average of fourteen thousand petitions a year, with the Chartist petition of 1842 alone accounting for 3 million signatures. Although it rarely hit these heights again, right up to the twentieth century, petitioning continued to provide a key mechanism for abstracting opinion from place and forging new affiliations between distant strangers.

Political movements underwent a similar transformation. When these first emerged between the Wilkite movement of the 1760s and Chartism in the 1840s, their national coherence depended heavily upon charismatic leaders like John Wilkes and Feargus O'Connor. At the height of the Wilkite movement in 1769, fifty thousand signed petitions and further pledges of support came from a variety of existing clubs, lodges, and associations from across much of England.[10] What bound them together was Wilkes himself and his personification of the causes of liberty: freedom of election, freedom of the press, and the right to publish parliamentary debates. Supporters sent him gifts, portraits were printed, his image was placed on mugs and plates, toasts were drunk to and pubs named after him, celebrations were held on his birthday. The extra-local nature of the movement was effectively held together by his personality and reputation. State repression in the form of the Seditious Meetings Act (1794), the Treason Acts (1795 and 1817), the Combinations Acts (1799, 1800, 1825), and the Six Acts (1819) necessarily blunted the organizational innovations of the Corresponding and Constitutional Societies of the 1790s and 1810s, which, like the political unions during the reform crisis of 1829–32, remained dependent upon individual leaders to knit them together as national movements—the litany of the names Paine, Cartwright, Cobbett, and Hunt says it all.[11] Incessant movement and tours around the country enabled these leaders to tie together divergent local struggles and organizations. In a single month during the Chartist agitation of 1839, O'Connor reportedly traveled fifteen hundred miles and spoke at twenty-two public meetings—often for several hours.[12] This type of charismatic organization was also enhanced by newspapers. Just as Wilkes had the *North Briton* and Cobbett his *Political Register,* O'Connor had the *Northern Star.* The *Northern Star* sold forty thousand copies by 1839 and claimed a readership of three hundred thousand. Its format—which combined reporting on the local activities of Chartist groups, covering national politics, letters from its readers, and sensationalist crime stories—proved very effective at connecting the dots of the movement.[13]

Despite the continuing importance of charismatic modes of organization, bureaucratic representative structures became increasingly essential for national political mobilization. The national reach and formal organizational structure of Chartism far outstripped its predecessors. By the late 1840s more than a thousand localities had had some form of Chartist organization, and between 1839 and 1858 these local branches sent delegates to the annual convention of the National Charter Association. The National Association was funded by a quarterly subscription of two pence, and membership cards were issued to men and women alike.[14] Yet it was the Anti-Corn Law League that led the way. Like the Chartists in 1839, it established a national convention for delegates elected by their local associations, and this developed a formal constitution (at its peak in 1842, 124 of the 316 local associations sent delegates). Funded by donations and the fund-raising activities of local associations, the league established a headquarters with fifteen full-time lecturers and a staff of twenty. By 1843 that staff was capable of distributing a million pamphlets a week in addition to the weekly *Anti-Corn Law Circular.* They also developed a nationally conceived electoral strategy, targeting specific candidates and constituencies as well as voters using the new electoral register created in 1832. Five million printed packets of tracts were sent to half a million voters in two hundred constituencies, either by post or delivered by hand, door to door, by five hundred distributors. Taking advantage of the Penny Post, the league mailed three hundred thousand letters a week directly to specifically selected voters. This was an unprecedented and formidable political machine.[15]

The Anti-Corn Law League anticipated the national organization of political parties that emerged twenty years later. The dramatic expansion of the electorate in 1867 and 1884 created more than 4 million new voters whose loyalty and support political parties now had to compete for. They did so by creating central organizations capable of mobilizing local associations in the constituencies. Firstly, the Conservative Central Office (1870) and the Liberal Central Association (1874)—which had been preceded by the Liberal Registration Association (1860)—began to coordinate and then direct party campaigning. Their influence was measured by the growth of a new cadre of professional party agents and centrally produced election literature. With their own professional organizations and journals specific to each party, agents became the central party's "fixers" on the ground, responsible for getting voters registered and organizing the growing ranks of party volunteers. At the advent of the twentieth century the Tories had more than four hundred agents, with the Liberals not far behind at 321. Created in 1887, the Liberal Publication Department produced 10 million leaflets for the 1892 election and 25 million at the next election just three years later. By 1910, albeit with two elections held that year, the Liberals distributed 40 million leaflets to the 46 million of the Conservative Central Office, amounting to a total of 10.75 leaflets for every one of 8 million deluged voters. Posters were also centrally produced, with both parties accounting for more than 5 million posted in 1910 alone, although these did not eradicate fly-posting of smaller and cheaper local posters.[16] Greater central party discipline was also apparent in the herding of party votes with the three-line whip in a Parliament that slowly lost its once cherished independent members.[17]

These strong central organs of power were to be held accountable, rhetorically at least, by a mass membership organized through local associations that were represented at an annual conference. The Conservative Party led the way with the creation of the National Union of Conservative Associations in 1867 as an umbrella for local associations (forty-four of which had been formed by 1873). Established a decade later, the National Liberal Federation had only seventy-seven local associations by 1880, but there were more than two hundred by the end of the century.[18] Both parties held an annual conference for representatives of the local associations, but their job was to energize supporters rather than to listen to them—the Conservatives even celebrated their lack of a constitution. If the Liberals' original Birmingham caucus had required a subscription of 1 shilling (or 12 pennies) a year, it was not a criterion for membership elsewhere, where nominations or pledges of support were sufficient. Animated local associations with an active "membership" became especially important when the 1883 Corrupt Practices Act made parties reliant on the campaign work of their own volunteers. It is perhaps better to think of these volunteers more as party activists than members, for even in the most politicized of wards and constituencies their combined total did not exceed 10 percent of voters.[19] Despite their central affiliation, local associations retained much autonomy. Even local Liberal associations chose their own candidates, and local political traditions were so well defended that nationally uniform party colors were not consolidated until after the First World War. Indeed, national parties continued to have specific local and regional flavors, whether Conservatism in Lancashire, Labourism in Poplar and the West Riding, or Liberalism in the West country.

Charismatic leadership also remained an important ingredient of national party political organization. William Gladstone and Benjamin Disraeli dominated their respective parties at the precise moment they were developing national organizational structures. Gladstone's passionate oratory, the almost biblical portrayal of causes like the Bulgarian atrocities, his use of rail and telegraph to reach a broader national public, were no less a part of the organizational repertoire of the Liberal Party than the formal structures of the National Liberal Federation.[20] The same was true of Henry Hyndman's Social Democratic Federation and the Labour Party's pioneers Keir Hardie and Ramsay MacDonald.[21] And, of course, it is almost impossible to think of the women's suffrage movement, and its more radical wing in the Women's Social and Political Union from 1903, without thinking of the Pankhursts, who made leadership a collective family affair.[22]

The remaking of associational and political culture around increasingly formalized national organizations capable of connecting and mobilizing distant strangers owed much to the capacity of print to abstract opinion from place and disseminate it widely.[23] Print culture was central to the early modern foundations of Britain's civil society. It had fueled not only England's Reformation but the demand for news during the Thirty Years War and the Civil War during the 1620s to 1640s.[24] Although newsbooks had been in circulation since the early seventeenth century, they proliferated after 1688: London had nineteen newspapers publishing fifty-five editions a week, including the first-ever daily in 1709. By the middle of the eighteenth century many of these newspapers were distributed across the country via the Post Office—more than a million in 1763 and more than four and a half million by 1790. Norwich boasted the first provincial paper in 1701, but by 1760 thirty-five were being published elsewhere. Nonetheless, most of the country waited for the arrival of news on the London mail coach.[25] At the start of the eighteenth century just 2.5 million newspapers were sold each year, but by its end that figure had risen to 17 million, with the most rapid growth coming in the last decade with an increase of 3 million occurring in 1792 and 1793 alone. Once again the big jump came in the nineteenth century. By 1844 there were nearly fifty-five thousand newspapers sold. Because papers were read aloud in company or shared in reading rooms, that was a fraction of their actual circulation—it was estimated that every London newspaper was read by thirty people in the 1820s. Yet although London's daily newspapers like *The Times* and *Morning Chronicle* claimed national circulations, it could still take them two days to reach Manchester in the 1840s. It was not until 1900, when the *Daily Mail* was simultaneously printed in London and Manchester, that any daily paper reached a national circulation of more than a million. By 1939 nearly all other national dailies had followed suit with dual printings, enabling them to reach a total circulation of 11.5 million papers, with 69 percent of the population older than sixteen reading one.[26]

The arrival of a national press was accompanied by the growth of provincial alternatives that served to reembed news in its local setting. There had been one weekly provincial paper in 1701, but by 1854 there were 289, and by 1907 there were 1,338 (with more than a hundred of those dailies). They grew steadily but unspectacularly between 1760 and 1847, from 35 to 230. By the 1840s Liverpool had no fewer than twelve of its own papers, while the Manchester *Guardian* and Leeds *Mercury,* which sold nine thousand copies (each of which reputedly reached between fifty and eighty readers), acquired a national reputation. These provincial papers reflected the still profoundly local nature of civil society; they carried detailed reports of the activities of local clubs, societies, and philanthropic associations as well as meetings by political organizations and official bodies like vestries, courts, and town councils. They also had a distinct voice and a steadfastly local angle of vision that refused to reproduce the contents of the London papers. After the Repeal of the Stamp Act in 1855 their numbers rapidly escalated: there were 938 in 1877 and 1,338 by 1907. This was the golden age of the provincial paper, with every city boasting papers that reflected political divisions and dynasties unique to the locality. Mancunians alone could read twenty-three local papers in the 1870s. It was only after the First World War that the numbers of provincial papers began to slowly decline (between 1921 and 1947 their numbers fell from 1,915 to 1,262), as they competed with the new forms of the national press and the advent of local radio.[27]

The press also became part of an imperial news system that conveyed news to distant subjects across the empire. Since the early nineteenth century, some colonies had developed their own English-language newspapers, and these eventually arrived by mail in Britain, where their contents were regurgitated in the London and provincial press. Even by the 1850s it took three months for news to travel to or from Australia, although steam ships reduced that to forty-five days until the advent of the telegraph in the 1870s. Telegraph rates were so prohibitive that as late as 1914 a prominent journalist complained that it was no longer the "geographical obstacle of distance" but commercial interests that prevented the diffusion of news and ideas across the empire. The London-based news agency Reuters was one of those

vested interests. Its cartel agreements had carved out a virtual monopoly upon news transmission across an imperial network that ran to fifty
offices and more than two hundred staff by 1906.[28] The Empire Press
Union was founded in 1909 to help foster imperial fellowship through
the exchange of news between the English-language press—by 1905
Sydney had four dailies, Wellington and Auckland two each, Cape
Town three, Pretoria three, Salisbury two, Kingston two, Calcutta six,
Madras four, Toronto six, Hong Kong and Shanghai four each.[29] If
there was an imperial civil society it was made possible by these newspapers and the newsreels and radio broadcasting that followed. This
was apparent during the First World War when the British state
assumed control of the Topical newsreel company and established the
Imperial Wireless Scheme through the Post Office. By 1932 the British
Broadcasting Corporation had established the Empire Service with a
network of shortwave relay stations across the empire.[30] Just as print
culture had during the eighteenth and nineteenth centuries, so broad-
cast media made it possible to imagine a civil society of distant strangers by abstracting opinion from person and place.

The invention of opinion polls provided the final abstraction of civil
society. The idea of a public opinion had existed since the late eighteenth century, but the eventual arrival of universal suffrage after 1918
generated a new hunger to understand it so as to better lead and direct
the fledgling demos. Politicians and journalists then believed that their
personal encounters with the public gave them an almost intuitive
understanding of its opinions. Moreover, public opinion was not then
the referent of politics; politicians felt their job was to lead, not follow it.
When new sampling techniques and tracking surveys—drawn in part
by Gallup's methods in the United States—were deployed to measure
morale in the Second World War, British public opinion became quan-
tifiable. The new reality and credibility of opinion polls arrived when
Mass Observation and Gallup famously called the 1945 election result
against the conventional wisdom of politicians and journalists. Within
two years the British Market Research Society and American Associa-

tion for Public Opinion Research were founded, and within the space of little more than a decade or two, opinion polls and quantitative approaches to measuring public opinion occupied a central place in the experience and understanding of the political process. Once embodied in person and place, in the balance of argument and contention, opinion became abstracted in numerical forms in which the identification of a majority view became paramount.[31]

Only a fool would suggest that even in the twentieth century civil society was entirely reorganized around abstract forms or bureaucratic structures. Electrical amplification and instantaneous replay of sound, as well as their capture on radio and newsreel films, made the interwar years a golden age of the mass demonstration and powerful oratory. The National Unemployed Workers Movement certainly took advantage of both the old tradition of mobilization and its new technological possibilities. Its national hunger marches started with small brigades leaving the furthest corners of the country and gathering the support of others as they converged upon a final demonstration in Hyde Park that attracted one hundred thousand people in 1932. Similarly, charismatic organization remained vital for Oswald Mosely's British Union of Fascists in the 1930s and Richard Acland's Commonwealth Party in the early 1940s. Yet it was the increasingly exceptional nature of these forms of political organization that is most apparent. Political culture, like associational life more broadly, had been fundamentally restructured during the preceding century or so as they adapted to the new challenges of operating in a society of strangers and an expanding imperial polity. Print culture allowed for the imagination of communities of sentiment and affinity that stretched beyond the local and personal. Yet these were ultimately sustained and mobilized by increasingly formal and bureaucratic modes of organization that were highly effective in binding together distant strangers. If much of this had germinated in the eighteenth century, it had clearly sprouted by the 1830s and was well established by the 1880s; so much so that by the 1930s it was possible to imagine the public as so many abstract statistics. Nonetheless, these increasingly abstract and bureaucratic ways of organizing civil society in some ways reanimated local and personal forms of association and political culture.

REPRESENTING STRANGERS

The same dialectic was apparent as Britain's electoral system was reformed in ways that made it appropriate for a society of strangers. In place of the distinct voting qualifications of each constituency and an understanding of the vote as a corporate responsibility, a new nationally uniform set of qualifications and an individuated electoral subject was created. This reanimated those who believed that it was communities, not individuals, that should be represented, for at issue was whether the power of the vote should be exercised secretly and anonymously or whether electors should be held personally accountable to their local communities.

Britain's electoral system had grown in fits and starts since the thirteenth century. Many constituencies, as well as their division into rural counties and urban boroughs, were literally medieval. In 1831 more than half of the boroughs (125 of 202) had been enfranchised by Edward I, while the 40-shilling freehold qualification for county voters had been set in 1430. These ancient representative mechanisms gained new significance in the seventeenth century as Parliament assumed a more central place in the structure of government, and inflation in property values swelled the electorate to three hundred thousand (6.6 percent of the population) by 1660. Yet elections during the seventeenth century had a confused and experimental character: there was uncertainty about who could vote, votes were cast in a myriad of ways, and elections were not won simply by having a majority of votes. Given that before 1642 almost no constituency had contested elections (in 1614, for example, just 14 of the 240 constituencies had contests), that was hardly surprising. Processes of selection—in which local aristocrats selected candidates who were then returned unopposed—far outweighed those of election.[32] Even though uncontested elections still outnumbered contested ones by a ratio of 2 to 1, as the electorate in England and Wales almost doubled in size from 240,000 to 439,200 between 1689 to 1831 (although outstripped by population growth, it declined as a percentage of adult males), the electoral process was codified around the representation of interests and communities.[33] This was evident from the range of different qualifications to vote as well as from the practices that surrounded the courting, casting, and counting of votes—both of which became a target for reformers in the nineteenth century.

The unreformed electoral system had a plethora of electoral qualifications that reflected a diverse and somewhat plastic conception of representation. In the rural counties all those with freehold property worth 40 shillings a year could vote, but in the urban boroughs one got to vote in a variety of ways: by being a member of the corporation (either selected or elected), by occupying specific properties, by paying poor rates, or by being a freeman (either from inheritance, occupational right, or as a gift of the corporation). Although these qualifications enfranchised different types (across the social scale) and numbers of voters, they all sought to represent the town through specific communities of people—the aldermen, the freemen, the propertied, or the inhabitants. For all its variety, the unreformed system had a common conception that the political subject it represented was corporate and communal.[34]

And this was very much evident in the conduct of elections. Candidates were routinely expected to nurse the constituency by "treating" the community as a whole through anything from holding lavish entertainments, making charitable donations, or hiring "campaign" workers. What was later termed "corrupt practices" was widely considered to be the natural and legitimate ways in which candidates showed their commitment and support for the community they sought to represent. Indeed, it was the community as a whole, not just the voters, that was canvassed to discover whether candidates had enough support to force or avoid a contest. Once a contest was formally declared, at a frequently dramatic and well-attended nomination ceremony open to the entire community, weeks of campaigning gave way to days of polling. Campaigns were boisterous affairs—full of speeches, noisy processions, dinners, and an endless stream of election literature posted at every available site. Competing candidates went to enormous lengths to get out their voters (or to prevent the opposition from doing so), and although voters were certainly prepared to sell their votes to the highest bidder, they did so within a cultural economy in which they were recognized as the vendors, not the ones being bought. All votes had first to be claimed and then publicly declared on a centrally constructed hustings below which those without the vote gathered to voice their approval or disapproval. Many believed that electors held their vote on trust from some broader group—their local communities, their occupations, their parties, or their families—that they were supposed to virtually represent. This was reaffirmed by the publication of poll books that carefully recorded who had voted for whom so that electors could be held accountable for how they had exercised their public trust.

The Reform Act of 1832 began a process that slowly but decisively transformed Britain's electoral system. The act did not dramatically increase the size of the electorate across the United Kingdom: it rose from 516,000 to 813,000 (or from 5 to 7 percent of the population), and much of that the initial growth faded within a generation as those who had qualified under the old system were grandfathered in to the new one until their deaths. Yet it inscribed a new concept of representation that was reflected in the uniformity and regularity of the system. It sought to take account of the country's mobile and growing population by redistributing seats from the now less populated south (where infamously towns like Dulwich and Old Sarum had effectively disappeared, leaving a dozen or so voters to return two members of Parliament [MPs]) to the north (where rapidly growing centers like Manchester, Birmingham, and Leeds, for instance, had no MPs). Although the use of double- and single-member constituencies sought to address huge discrepancies in size, there still remained thirty-five constituencies with fewer than thirty-five voters, compared to Liverpool's eleven thousand.

This was not an attempt to equalize the ratio of voters to MPs so that each claimed the same representative power. It sought instead to represent nations, communities, and interests. Thus Scotland and Ireland were afforded more MPs, and the sixty-five new seats for urban boroughs were offset by sixty-five new county seats to safeguard aristocratic interests.

The Reform Act also enshrined a new type of political subject around standardized qualifications to vote. Firstly, unlike legislation in 1818, 1819, and 1831 that had allowed women to vote in parish vestry elections, it designated for the first time that voters could be "male persons only"—a precedent followed with the New Poor Law and Municipal Reform Acts of 1834 and 1835. Secondly, new uniform limits were set on residency qualification (a year for the parliamentary franchise, two and a half years for the municipal one), while those who had received poor relief two and a half years before the election were disqualified from voting. Thirdly, the single uniform standard of the £10 householder qualification replaced the various borough franchises of the unreformed system.[35] At the municipal level, where a similar profusion of representative systems existed, the Municipal Reform Act of 1835 lodged the right to vote with all male ratepayers resident for three years—a standard enforced upon 178 existing corporations and adopted by a further (usually rapidly growing and industrializing) sixty-two towns and cities. This standardization of franchises displaced customary local definitions of who should be represented and why with a national norm. A new type of political subject was born—*men* who possessed the vote by virtue of their *property*, which it was believed bestowed upon them the independence of thought to vote as *individuals*.

The electoral process was reshaped around this new political subject. The creation of an Electoral Register in 1832 ensured that electors' right to vote was tested in court before the election, not on the hustings during it. The parish overseer compiled lists of ratepayers which were then collated and published by the constituency's returning officer, with any objections heard by revising barristers in court. The act of voting was also transformed. The length of the poll was reduced to just sixteen hours over two days (it had been reduced to eight days in 1828), and because a hustings now had to be built for every six hundred electors, it ceased to be a site where the entire community could gather and hold electors accountable for their votes. Indeed, increasing efforts were made to insulate electors from the "undue influences" that became defined as "corruption." In effect, any influence was undue, because electors were now to vote according to their own opinions and conscience. Various bills against corruption were moved and defeated in Parliament (1806, 1814, 1818, 1832, 1841, 1842), but they helped codify and define the "corrupt practices" outlawed in 1854: polling was reduced to a single day, election expenses were officially audited, and fines were introduced for bribery, treating, and intimidation. These were extended further in 1883 when the employment of election workers was effectively prohibited, limits were placed on election expenses, and harsher penalties (including imprisonment and exclusion from voting or holding public office for seven years) were introduced. Within the space of a generation, a new understanding of corruption had transformed the practice of elections and insulated voters as individuals from forms of "undue influence" once considered natural and appropriate.[36] It marked a decisive shift away from an electoral process rooted in local and communal relations of personal accountability to one better suited for an anonymous society of strangers.

Nowhere was this more apparent than with the introduction of the secret ballot. The New Poor Law and the Municipal Corporations Acts began the experiment with different types of voting in private. Ballot cards that varied locally in design were distributed to electors at home, who returned them completed in person or by post, or that were then collected two days later by paid agents. Privacy, not secrecy, was the issue. The secret ballot was first introduced for school board elections in 1870, with municipal and parliamentary elections following in 1872.[37] Following the Australian model practiced since 1856, new private polling booths were designed that guaranteed both the secrecy of the vote

and (eventually) the anonymity of the voter. A new sanctity and deco-
rum surrounded the act of voting. Polling places—one every 4 miles
with one booth for every 150 electors—contained clear instructions
that electors had to keep their vote secret and leave as soon as they had
voted, and anyone found "interfering" with voters would be immedi-
ately removed. Despite some protest that this was all too unmanly and
un-English, the act was passed for an initial eight years and was thereafter annually renewed. At the 1880 election some thirty-five thousand
voters declared themselves illiterate and had their ballots marked by a
polling clerk (thus violating the secrecy of their vote), but generally
there were remarkably few teething problems and the secret ballot was
made permanent in 1918. Voting in secret—so long an anathema to an
electoral culture orientated around face-to-face relations with a doc-
trine of virtual representation and public accountability—had finally
been naturalized.

Nonetheless, this new conception of the voter as an individuated
and anonymous political subject remained haunted by the ghostly presence of the corporate ethos and personal relations of the old electoral
system. Far from eradicating the politics of influence, the secret ballot
sought "to preserve it in an acceptable and legitimate form."[38] Certainly, factory owners in small towns, like landlords of rural estates,
continued to march their voting employees to the poll and to treat them
with parties, picnics, holidays, and festivals. Well into the twentieth
century, aristocratic families, like the Derbys in Lancashire, continued
to serve as patrons to constituencies spreading their largesse in ways
that were intended to cement their influence—providing a building
here, a park there. Still, 20–30 percent of seats remained uncontested
after 1872, and it was only after 1918 that constituencies were legally
obliged to stage contests. A more modest politics of influence also continued on the borderlines of the new anticorruption legislation. The
heightened authority of party agents after 1883 relied in good measure
on their knowledge of electoral law and how to bend it. Denied the
opportunity to "hire" party workers, the nursing of constituencies grew

in significance, with prospective candidates able to make donations to local charities and support local events—while sitting members were free to do so at all times outside of election campaigns. Before World War I there were reputedly as many as twenty-eight constituencies, mainly in small southern boroughs, renowned for their corruption, where the old ways died hard. Even in the 1950s the local Tory candidate would visit my grandfather's pub in Sussex and buy a round of drinks or two for the assembled clientele. Neither the secret ballot nor the Corrupt Practices Act eradicated the politics of influence. An electoral culture that had sought to balance corporate influence and interests became imbricated in a reformed system designed to insulate and individuate voters.

That this corporate ethos was not simply a surviving remnant of the unreformed system was further evident when the Redistribution Act of 1885 failed to impose single-member constituencies (twenty-four double-member constituencies were maintained). The act did not meet the demands of those who advocated for proportional representation or equal electoral districts in order to ensure that each vote had an equivalent weight and value. Neither did it satisfy those who resisted the breaking apart of double-member constituencies that represented meaningful historical communities. Outside of large cities that were divided fairly arbitrarily into a series of roughly proportional subdivisions, the corporate model of representing specific communities prevailed; hence the still-considerable variations in size of both single- and double-member constituencies. This corporate model of representation, bolstered by the communal social theories of Henry Maine and the idealists during the 1870s and 1880s, was again entrenched by the Representation of the Peoples Act of 1918.[39] The act that introduced universal manhood suffrage and votes for women over age thirty retained ten double-member constituencies and wildly different sizes of single-member constituencies to reflect their historical integrity as communities. It also retained and extended certain forms of plural voting in the shape of the business and university franchises.[40] Thus the university franchise, which allowed graduates of an expanding list of universities to elect their own members while also voting in their "home" constituencies, expanded as twenty-one universities were afforded fifteen seats and the vote was extended to all graduates (not just those in possession of master of arts degrees). Even the advent of universal manhood suffrage was balanced by the privileging of proper corporate interests weighted by property and education.[41]

The reanimation of a corporate or communal model of representation was also evident in late colonial societies. In India the representative system, cautiously introduced in 1909 and further developed in 1919 and 1935 (by which time the electorate had grown to 30 million, a sixth of the adult male population), was designed around representing communities—of religion, caste, and tribe—that the British thought structured Indian society through the creation of separate electorates with reserved seats. This allowed the balancing of the interests of these communities with the influence of princely rulers and representatives nominated by imperial officials in ways that also punctured the unity of nationalists pushing for further reform or independence.[42] It was a model transported to Kenya during the 1920s and 1930s where it produced separate electorates and representative systems for white settlers, Arabs, Indians, and a limited number of Africans. Indeed, there were five separate electorates just for Indians alone! A very similar approach was taken to the systems of communal representation, structured by tribe and region, that were instantiated by the various constitutions produced in British Nigeria from 1921 through to 1957, which also, as in India, continued to hold a place for representatives "selected" by the governor, chiefs, and native authorities.

Significantly, late colonial electoral systems also drew upon the newly individuated forms of British electoral culture. David Gilmartin has highlighted how from 1919, Indian electoral law, framed around similar distinctions between natural and undue influences upon individual voters, included provision for the secret ballot and borrowed wholesale the terms (as well as the title) of the corrupt practices legislation of 1883. The aim was for electors to vote as individuals, protected from the undue influences of bribery and corruption, but to do so as representatives of particular communities. To achieve this the provinces adopted one of two voting systems, both of which violated the secrecy of the vote: one allowed polling clerks to help those who declared themselves illiterate to vote, the other used color-coded ballot boxes for each candidate. Although these systems were later adopted across the late colonial empire—the former in Nigeria, Uganda, Kenya, British Guiana, Zanzibar, and Sudan, the latter in Tanganyika and the Gold Coast—neither appeared to successfully individuate the voter. British officials in Tanganyika during the late 1950s were thus frustrated that their attempts to modernize the country's representative system through the secret ballot failed to eradicate the corporate loyalties of the electorate.[43] Yet, as we have seen, the tension between the communal and the individuated form of the political subject was no colonial confection; it came directly from the British model even if it was buttressed by a particular colonial sociology.

•   •   •

Today the leaders of the West often suggest that only those who practice a particular model of democracy can lay claim to being modern. Yet, as this account of the development of Britain's civil society and electoral system makes clear, democracy in the West arose in culturally and historically specific contexts, and the contingency, particularity, and historicity of their forms have largely been forgotten.[44] Rather than a history of heroic liberal reformers or of a ideological contest between different theories of political representation, I have sought to show how the politics of association and representation were remade in ways that allowed them to operate in a society of strangers and an expanding imperial polity. This is not a causal claim. I am not arguing that the new abstract and bureaucratic ways of reorganizing civil society and electoral politics in Britain were simply caused by the increasing size of its population and empire. I am suggesting that these conditions not only posed new challenges to forms of association and representation that until the eighteenth century had primarily been mediated through local and personal relations but also provided new constraints on and possibilities for how distant strangers could be imagined, organized, and represented as political subjects. Clearly this did not happen overnight, or in a day, month, year, or even decade. If the late eighteenth and early nineteenth centuries saw the first systematic moves toward a more formalized, impersonal, and extra-local civil society, it was the period between the 1830s and 1880s that they really took hold, even if they were still being consolidated in the first half of the twentieth century. So much so that we have repeatedly seen how local and personal forms of association and representation were reanimated in myriad ways by charismatic political leaders, the provincial press, and corporate understandings of the electoral system.

CHAPTER FIVE

An Economy of Strangers

Britain's modernity has often been tied to a single event: the Industrial Revolution. Eric Hobsbawm described it as no less than "the most fundamental transformation of human life in the history of the world recorded in written documents."[1] And few doubted that this world historical event happened first in Britain. This was not solely a national conceit. Overseas observers like Jean-Baptiste Say and Jerome Blanqui created the term *industrial revolution* to capture the economic transformations in Britain during the 1820s and 1830s, while Marx also highlighted the unique historical form of industrial capitalism there.[2] Yet it was not until the 1880s that Arnold Toynbee made the term part of our common sense, using it to describe the mechanization of production, the division of labor, and the triumph of the cash nexus between 1780 and 1830. Ever since, economic historians have been asking why Britain was first, when and where it happened, and what were the nature and effects of its processes.[3] This impressive body of scholarship invariably assumes that not only did the Industrial Revolution usher in the modern world, but that it determined the shape of our modern social and political conditions.

In contrast, I follow those who have reversed the explanatory tide by positing that changing patterns of social organization were the harbinger of the great economic transformation that became known as industrial capitalism.[4] Simply put, Adam Smith was wrong. He believed that the growth of commercial activity had created the society of strangers, whereas I suggest that the society of strangers restructured the practice of economic life. The rapid and sustained growth of an increasingly dispersed and urban population created new challenges for the conduct of economic life that had long revolved around local markets and face-to-face exchanges with people one knew and trusted. To facilitate transactions between strangers and across distance, market information was abstracted from people and place through print. In addition, through print the forms of exchange—whether the legal status of companies, or the use of money or weights and measures—were standardized so that relations of trust were transferred from *whom* one did business with to *how* that business was conducted. Just as these processes transformed the practice of economic life, so they made it possible to imagine markets as part of a single entity called "the economy" that was endowed with systemic qualities and projected upon different national and international spaces.

Nonetheless, personal relationships, like local and regional networks of trade and association, remained important to markets into the twentieth century. This was, perhaps, especially true of labor and capital markets where small-scale hand-craft production persisted alongside factory paternalism, and relations of credit and capital investment continued to draw upon personal ties, reputations, and relationships. Rather than simply the relics of a bygone era, these were attempts to repersonalize exchange relations in response to the increasingly anonymous and abstract nature of economic life. The new forms of economic life that we came to know as industrial capitalism, then, simultaneously estranged and abstracted practices of exchange from social relations and then embedded them in new ones that appeared to take surprisingly "traditional" forms.

ABSTRACTING MARKETS FROM PERSON AND PLACE

Markets had been around for centuries before 1750. Although most were embedded in specific places and animated through personal relationships—one invariably knew whom one traded with, invested in, borrowed money from, or worked for—intercontinental trade between strangers was not unknown in the early modern period. Because transportation by sea or land was slow and expensive, this trade was largely confined to high-value and low-weight goods like silk, spices, or diamonds. Diasporic or nomadic merchant groups who trusted their own kin, as well as political and physical infrastructures that protected and housed traders along well-established trade routes, made this type of intercontinental trade between strangers possible. Locally specific legal systems and tribunals enabled the development of conventions that helped regulate the nature of partnerships between family members and fellow investors just as the sharing of market information and incentives facilitated transactions between merchants and their distant agents. Yet although it has been suggested that "the birth of impersonal exchange" or "anonymous capitalism" occurred in the late medieval period, its scale remained remarkably modest in comparison to that of the eighteenth and nineteenth centuries.[5]

Intercontinental and interregional trade first began to flourish in Britain during the late seventeenth century. Wool continued to be the chief export to the continent, but Britain's expanding imperial networks across the Atlantic world and through to Asia enabled the rapid growth of new imported commodities (like sugar, tobacco, and calicoes), much of which was then reexported to Europe or, as with the case of slaves, exported directly to the Caribbean and Americas from Africa.[6] This was made possible by the flow of silver bullion from the Americas, but it also relied upon the extension of commercial networks both by joint stock companies granted a royal monopoly for trade in a particular region—like the Levant Company (1580), the East India Company (1599), the Hudson's Bay Company (1670), the Royal African Company (1672), and the South Sea Company (1711)—and by merchants. It was these merchants and companies that developed innovative systems for organizing long-distance trade and managing what economists describe as the principal-agent problem—that is, creating systems and incentives that ensured that distant agents acted in the interests of their employers.

Until the creation of road and canal networks in the second half of the eighteenth century, interregional trade within Britain was limited to commodities like wool, coal, and grain that could be shipped along the coastal and inland river networks. As the speed of transporting goods increased and costs declined, merchants were able to extend the geographical reach of their trade in ways that transformed how markets operated. Take the grain trade. It had long been customary for farmers to take their harvest to the nearest market where local millers, retailers, and inhabitants could inspect it before purchase. These local markets often regulated who could buy and when—with inhabitants coming first, then millers, and finally retailers and merchants—to ensure that those who could purchase in large quantities did not effectively price townspeople out of the market. In the second half of the eighteenth century, as the price of transporting grain over greater distances dropped and the urban population grew, farmers and merchants began to dominate what had become a seller's market. Instead of transporting all their grain to market for locals to inspect its quality and quantity, farmers bought small samples for inspection, knowing this was enough for millers and merchants buying large quantities for sale outside of the locality, wherever a better price might be had. This helped catalyze a whole new cash economy: unlike sales to local inhabitants, where payment was made in kind or by cash and token, farmers received from merchants new forms of paper money that were deposited in banks that then recirculated it to others as credit.[7]

The transition to markets characterized by cash exchanges and long-distance trade did not, though, herald the arrival of impersonal forms of exchange. For those who traded in commodities, stocks, or financial services during the seventeenth and eighteenth centuries, the market was not an abstract space but a particular place where personal relationships, reputations, and knowledge was critical. Built in the late sixteenth century at the heart of the City of London, the Royal Exchange was *the* place where merchants went to participate in Britain's burgeoning interregional and intercontinental trade networks. So congested and varied had the commercial life of the exchange become by the eighteenth century that specific areas of it as well as its surrounding streets became associated with trade in particular commodities or regions. Merchants had to know who traded in what and where. In gaining access to these intricate circuits of knowledge, a merchant's reputation preceded him. If he was considered trustworthy and reliable—that is, his commercial intelligence was accurate and useful, the quality of his goods assured, his credit sound—doors opened to the people, information, and credit necessary to trade. Despite the appearance of advice manuals that sought to explain the conventions and practices of the exchange, it remained structured by highly personal reputations, flows of information, and face-to-face relationships.[8]

The same was true of London's emergent stock market. Before 1688 the trade in shares of all fifteen joint stock companies was infrequent and conducted between individuals in private without the need for brokers. Thereafter, the scale of stock exchanges increased, with the number of joint stock companies rising to 150 by 1695 as new, large-scale domestic enterprises—like banks and water utilities—required larger reserves of capital.[9] Although the fledgling financial press began to record lists of stock prices, they were published so infrequently that investors and brokers relied upon a local culture of conversation for gleaning timely and accurate information for day-to-day trading.[10] The City of London's coffee houses and dense network of alleys and streets were vital propagators of this orally conveyed intelligence about stocks, prices, and more general knowledge about commodities and securities. Yet the promiscuous mix of urban strangers found there heightened anxiety about who could be trusted and catalyzed attempts to delineate the stock market as a specific place where access could be regulated. In 1761 a group of brokers rented Jonathan's Coffee House for three hours a day and demanded an annual subscription in return for membership and access to the market. By 1772 a purpose-built stock market, open to all for a daily fee, had been established in Sweetings Alley, but it failed to secure a monopoly of all trading (the Bank of England's Rotunda, for instance, remained central to the trade in securities). The final transition to a closed market came in 1801, when brokers had to pay a sizeable annual subscription of 10 guineas and observe the rules and regulations laid down by a governing body that vetted new members and clerks to ensure they were trustworthy.[11] Making the stock market a club to which membership was limited to those whose reputations had already been secured solved the problem of doing business with strangers. Certainly, Joel Mokyr is right that in 1800 capital markets "were still based on personal relationships and reputations," but they had already begun to be formalized and systematized.[12]

Ironically, the stock market, with its dense network of personal networks and connections, had grown with the expansion of the company form—the joint stock company—most associated with a new type of impersonal exchange. Although after 1688 Parliament granted corporate status to joint stock companies only if it was deemed in the public interest to do so, this process was so onerous and expensive that a new type of unincorporated joint stock company, operating effectively as multiple partnerships, proliferated. It was these that were held responsible for the South Sea Bubble collapse and were outlawed in 1720. Over the next century joint stock companies continued to be criticized for encouraging speculative frenzies, monopolizing trade, and failing to ensure that their directors were liable for losses or accountable to shareholders in bankruptcy. When the repeal of the Bubble Act in 1825 unleashed fresh waves of boom-and-bust speculation, fueled by fraudulent promotions, the Companies Act of 1844 sought to protect investors by limiting the liabilities of companies in return for new standards of accountability. The apparent triumph of the long-reviled joint stock company form was not greeted with universal approbation. Many still believed they would eviscerate a commercial world held together by the personal bonds of trust and accountability evident in the partnership. As *The Times* lamented, it ushered in a society "in which friendship, ability, knowledge, education, character, credit, even monied worth is in great measure disregarded; and money, the mere amount and value of the shares standing in the name of each, is the sole bond of connection between proprietors."[13] The Companies Act sought to replace these personal forms of accountability by formal structures that made public companies legible to potential investors and shareholders alike, but this regulatory framework was rescinded in 1855 and, despite further revisions to company law in 1867 and 1890, it was not until 1900 that it again became compulsory for companies to publish audited accounts. No doubt this was driven by the widening circle (socially and geographically) of shareholders and the increasing size and complexity of public companies, which by 1901 had reached a total of six thousand. Nonetheless, this represented a tiny fraction of all British businesses: 95 percent were still private partnerships in 1885. *The Times*'s lament for the advent of impersonal, anonymous capitalism in 1844 had been somewhat premature.[14]

The management of those private companies also remained highly personalized. Textile mills and engineering factories had grappled with the organizational problems of large, complex, or geographically dispersed enterprises since the late eighteenth century. Innovative employers like Wedgewood, or Boulton and Watt, pioneered new systems of centralized production, new divisions of labor and wage structures, new time disciplines for workers, new forms of cost accounting and new standardized forms of production that enabled quality control—each of which was transferable across distance and between different plants. Although these techniques were celebrated in print from the 1830s, the vast majority of companies remained dominated by an owner-proprietor who favored personal, not systemic, forms of management.[15] Ideas of character and learning from experience on the job were central to the personal art of management. Owner-proprietors frequently trusted in people, not systems, appointing extended family members as managers of different plants, sometimes in conjunction with a trusted foreman or works manager. Business historians generally agree that there was a remarkable lack of innovation in British management styles or business organization until the early twentieth century. Enterprises, like the railways, that were geographically dispersed and had high levels of capital investment by those with no interest in managing the business, did systematize management with new types of cost and price control, delegation of responsibility to local and regional divisions, and frequent reporting of information up and down the system. German approaches to management as a science only registered in Britain after the merger mania of the late nineteenth and early twentieth centuries dramatically increased the size of many companies. Despite the enormous scale of armaments production coordinated by the Ministry of Munitions during the Great War and the emergence of new corporate giants like Imperial Chemical Industries (ICI) (1926) and Unilever (1930), it is worth remembering that as late as 1898 the average workplace employed just thirty people and by 1907 only one hundred firms had three thousand workers on their payrolls, accounting for a mere 5 percent of the total workforce.[16] When small private businesses remained the norm, it was hardly surprising that the management of companies remained highly personal.

Personal relations did not, then, just remain a key component of economic life through the nineteenth century; they were often formalized to account for the new conditions of living, working, and doing business in a society of strangers. As Joel Mokyr has observed, the character of the economy was profoundly altered between 1700 and 1850: "People not only bought their daily bread, clothing and houses, but also sold their labor and invested their savings through markets, in all aspects of economic life dealing with strangers."[17] There were many components to this but, as with the transformation of the state and civil society, print culture and new systems of communication were essential. New systems of communication—from writing letters to accounting and filing systems, to printed news and guides, to the telegraph and telephone—abstracted economic knowledge from place and person, disseminating it over greater distances at increasing speeds, in ways that allowed transactions to occur between strangers who would never meet.

Nowhere was this more evident than in financial markets. During the seventeenth century Europe's leading commercial cities—Amsterdam, Antwerp, Hamburg, and London— all published, sometimes in several languages, bills of entry (lists of imported commodities at their ports), price currents (commodity prices), marine lists (of ships and their cargoes), and exchange currents (rates on foreign bills of exchange)[18] London had its first bill of entry published in 1619, but when the state ceased licensing this information in 1695 there was a flowering of new publications by the coffee houses associated with marine business and the trade in stocks and securities: *Lloyd's News* (1696) was quickly followed by Garraway's *The Course of Exchange and Other Things* (1697). Published once or twice a week (and delivered by hand or post on subscription), these newssheets of prices and cargoes were not intended for habitués of the City's coffee houses involved in daily trade but for those further afield, including the North American colonies, who wanted to keep abreast.[19] Provincial ports and exchanges spawned their own price lists and bills of entry: Bristol from the 1740s and Liverpool from the 1760s, and these slowly became incorporated into local papers alongside more general "remarks on trade."[20] There was also a proliferation of guides and manuals published—particularly over that most thorny of issues of calculating rates of interest—for the aspiring businessman who wished to understand the opaque conventions of London's commercial and financial worlds.[21] Despite the increasing reach of printed commercial and financial news during the eighteenth century, the speed of its distribution meant that it remained a way of informing distant readers of market trends. Trading still required people to meet in actual markets.

It was only in the nineteenth century that print culture truly abstracted knowledge from the personal relations and physical place of the market. In the 1820s, the *Morning Chronicle* was the first to run regular "City reports" and was dutifully followed by the *Times*'s feature "Money, Market and City Intelligence," which became the authoritative source, largely thanks to the personal reputation of its financial editor Thomas Alsanger. Alongside these reports in the daily press came an increasing number of often short-lived specialist journals tailored around specific markets, like the *Circular to Bankers* (1828) or the *Estates Gazette* (1858).[22] As commercial and financial journalism moved from printing lists of information to describing market activity, it did not just abstract and disseminate information but ordered and interpreted it. *The Economist* illustrates this well. Founded as the organ of the Anti-Corn Law League in 1843, it provided the first bird's-eye view of all market activity that it understood as forming a single domain—"the economy." With a circulation peaking at less than 4,500 in 1847, the success and prestige of *The Economist* rested not on its popularity but the accuracy of its information and the shrewdness of its analysis. Both owed much to the reputation of its long-standing editor, Walter Bagehot, who had inherited the position in 1860 after the death of his father-in-law, its founder. Bagehot used his reputation and personal connections in the City to obtain knowledge of the market before abstracting and framing an understanding of it in print. Under his editorship *The Economist* developed price indices that tracked percentage changes in volume and value in ways that allowed the identification of trade cycles from the 1870s.[23]

By developing new ways of understanding markets, financial journalism did not just enable people to participate in them but also made those markets appear a natural part of the order of things. As the number of publicly floated companies and individual investors steadily increased in the late nineteenth century, new publications sought to make sense of an increasingly complex world of finance for businessmen and investors alike.[24] Alongside these weekly and daily newspapers came a plethora of manuals that sought to rationalize market behavior, explain speculative panics and crashes, and even teach *How to Read the Money Article*.[25] *Francis Playford*'s *Practical Hints for Investing Money* led the way. First published in 1855, it went to a second edition in 1856, was reissued in 1865 before being updated and republished in 1882 by his son Walter M. Playford as *Hints for Investors* in what was by then a crowded field.[26] Untouched by historians, this treasure trove of manuals did not just tame the market by presenting it as knowable, they produced a calculative subject: an investor who rationally comprehended the market and mapped its trends and regularities so as to profit from them.[27] Financial journalism, then, abstracted knowledge from the intimate physical place and personal relations of the market while also forging a common understanding of the market as a rational system that calculative investors could master.

Print culture also changed business organization and management, albeit more slowly. Although letter writing and double-entry book keeping had long been a feature of Europe's mercantile counting houses, from the late seventeenth century Britain's joint stock companies developed new mechanisms for managing overseas agents. Faced with the challenge of managing its agents along the Bay of Bengal when it took almost two years to complete a cycle of trade and reporting, the East India Company turned to standardized forms for stock taking and accounting to ensure that the operations of each agent and "factory" were accountable to company directors back in London.[28] Similarly, in the Caribbean and American colonies, plantation owners, especially absentee ones, developed accounting systems to track the productivity and value of their slaves.[29] By the late eighteenth century, systems for reporting units of production and sales, wage expenditures, as well as stock-taking and cost-accounting measures were in use by some large manufacturing companies in Britain. James Watt had even invented a copying press to create standardized reporting forms for his business. And yet, constrained by clerks or agents with neither the time nor the expertise to adopt new systems, ad hoc experiential methods specific to person and place continued to dominate management practice. It was not until the scale and complexity of companies increased in the 1880s, and the law increasingly mandated the publication of accounts for joint stock companies, that publications about management and accounting proliferated. These texts invariably provided sample forms and tables for use across the production process and between plants.[30] New office systems and technologies were developed in the nineteenth century that facilitated more systemic approaches to management: vertical filing replaced bound volumes of accounts and correspondence, the typewriter and carbon copying replaced writing and copy pressing, and the telephone enabled speedier long-distance communication between branches and plants.[31] The idea that commercial life could be organized around abstract principles and standardized practices that were transferable across space may have first been evident in the late seventeenth and eighteenth centuries, but it was only in the nineteenth century that it became disseminated and adopted more broadly through print.

CREATING THE NATIONAL ECONOMY

If print culture allowed market information and commercial practices to travel across distance by abstracting them from person and place, it was the state that carved out a flat, uniform, and homogenous national (and later imperial) space that facilitated economic transactions between strangers. This forging of a national economy was no less critical to state formation than the imagination and politicization of a national community, and it was achieved by creating new standardized forms of money and measurement.[32] These made it possible to transpose the problem of trust in whom you traded with onto the forms of inscription that made it possible for you to trade with those you did not know.

The cash nexus was hardly a modern invention: some exchange relations had been mediated by money for millennia. Nonetheless, money in its modern form, as a state produced, standardized, and transferable token whose worth exceeded the intrinsic value of its material, has a remarkably recent history. In early modern England, the Crown, through the Royal Mint, claimed a monopoly of the right to produce coins of the realm with a value guaranteed by their weight in silver and gold. Yet an almost continuous shortage of specie ensured that coins were not only worn but constantly clipped and filed (to say nothing of counterfeited), so that their value in weight was considerably less than their face value. Local corporations and tradesmen issued their own tokens of exchange as more reliable counterparts to the coin of the realm: in the 1660s there were 3,543 tokeners in London alone.[33] Credit relations proliferated within this chaotic cash nexus. Credit for local sales and services were invariably realized through face-to-face negotiations by which an economy of mutual obligation could be maintained.[34] Transactions between regions or overseas, where the transportation of coin was risky or impractical, relied upon new types of paper instruments like bills of exchange, promissory notes, and various types of bank notes. Leaving aside the hotly debated morality of an economy fueled by credit and paper money, there were widespread concerns about the reliability of these paper instruments given that all depended upon signatures that could be forged and signatories that might not be trustworthy.[35]

After 1688 the state sought to restore confidence and credibility in the cash economy. The formation of the Bank of England in 1694 provided a new solidity to paper money through its notes of credit (issued to those who had deposited bullion) that were backed by silver reserves and income from government loans. Arguing that if money was to become a reliable basis of exchange it had to correlate to its proper value in weight, John Locke and Sir Isaac Newton (as Warden of the Royal Mint) engineered the Great Recoinage of 1696 to restore all silver coins to their intrinsic value. Forgery was made a capital offense in 1697, and new techniques for milling coin and printing Bank of England notes made counterfeiting harder. Finally, with the Act of Union in 1707, the new system was extended to Scotland, which had to abandon its own separate currency.

The new regime struggled to take hold. It did not reach many remote areas like the Scottish highlands and the North American colonies, where tokens of nails, leather, and cards remained in circulation. Recoinage was also unpopular, provoking riots in London and Yorkshire and widespread avoidance of the window tax (designed to make good the deficit between the value of recovered and restored coins) by reducing the number of their windows.[36] The rush to secure new coins generated a shortage of silver that forced the Bank of England to suspend cash payments on its notes; by 1705 promissory notes had become so widespread that those under £20 were made legally transferable as cash.[37] Counterfeited, light, and foreign coins as well as tradesmen's tokens continued to circulate in large numbers. As paper notes became more common because of the shortages of silver coins, cases of forgery were more frequently reported in the press.[38] And, finally, the shortage of specie during the wars with revolutionary France led to a run on the banks that reduced the number of provincial banks from four hundred to just eight in 1793. Four years later, the Bank of England's deposits were so depleted that it suspended cash payments on its notes and issued paper currency in the form of £1 and £2 notes for the first time. Forgery of these notes was so rife that in an attempt to restore their credibility and the credibility of the cash economy more broadly, the bank launched a huge criminal investigation that at its apex in 1820 led to the well-publicized prosecution of more than four hundred forgers.[39]

Once again, the debate about how to restore credibility and trust in Britain's monetary system was rehearsed. While the Bank of England had been partially restoring its bullion deposits after suspension, the Bullion Committee of 1811 outlined a new commitment to pegging the currency solely to gold (rather than the bi-metal standard that had been sufficient for Locke and Newton) after the cessation of hostilities. Another recoinage followed in 1816, but though it restored gold coins to their proper weight and intrinsic value, it allowed the smaller denominations of copper and silver coins to be issued at their extrinsic face value. This was made possible by Boulton's new steam-powered Royal Mint, which, by ensuring the uniformity of these coins in ways unattainable by the preceding hand-hammered methods, finally put the counterfeiters out of business and allowed tradesmen's tokens to be outlawed in 1812. By 1821, with the Bank of England bullion deposits fully restored, the value of its notes was pegged to gold. Finally it seemed the security, stability, and trust in a uniform monetary system had been established.

In reality it remained prone to several pressures. Reformers like William Cobbett railed against the deflation and unemployment caused by the creation of the gold standard and at every downturn called for it to be abandoned. Free traders like Attwood and Cobden also refused the fiction that gold was the natural and ancient basis of the currency and dreamt of a cosmopolitan alternative that would facilitate freedom of trade and movement.[40] The idea was influential enough that the economists W. S. Jevons and Robert Lowe (Gladstone's chancellor between 1868 and 1873) seriously considered a variety of schemes for international currency standardization, discussions that culminated in 1865 with the "Latin Union" of France, Switzerland, Italy, and Belgium sharing the franc.[41] Domestically the monetary system was also under such strain that a series of Bank Acts between 1826 and 1844 reduced the numbers of banks that could issue notes and ensured that notes had to correspond to their bullion deposits. Although the Bank of England issued only printed notes of fixed denomination after 1855, thirty years later they were still competing with notes issued by just shy of 150 banks. Similarly, despite a series of recoinages (in 1870, 1889, and 1891), gold coins continued to wear and be clipped—in 1890, 45 percent of gold sovereigns were "light."[42]

Arguably, money did not finally reach its uniform, modern form until the Great War. It was only in 1917 that all coins were made tokens with an easily maintained face-value, and four years later Bank of England secured a monopoly on the right of issuing notes. This was not as late as it seems. The United States of America, which had spent several decades after independence trying to establish its own currency and central bank, was by the 1830s struggling to manage a chaotic monetary system that contained sixteen hundred local banks issuing notes that with more than thirty thousand varieties of design were so easily forged a third of all currency was considered counterfeit before the creation of national bank notes in 1866. Their design and production was slowly centralized, culminating in the establishment of the Federal Reserve in 1913 and the standardization of all notes in 1929. In the British case, the essential components of the gold standard and a uniform monetary system was in place by the 1840s, even if it took several more decades for that system to be stabilized. Locke's and Newton's vision of money as an impersonal and trustworthy unit of exchange had been finally realized, and in the process the cash economy had been remade for a society of strangers. One no longer had to trust the bearer of the note or coin, for the state had guaranteed the universal value of all money.

Given how difficult it was to secure a uniform monetary system in Britain, it is unsurprising that attempts to extend that across the empire were frustrated. After Britain had gone on to the gold standard, a series of imperial orders in the mid-1820s sought to secure the pound as a transcolonial currency (in Australia, Canada, the Cape Colony, West Indies and, a little later, New Zealand). Many of these colonies, like India, continued to have a bewildering variety of coins and tokens. There, locally specific systems of value and exchange ensured that hundreds of different types of gold, silver, copper, lead, and tin coins existed alongside tokens like sea shells *(cauris)* and bitter almonds *(badams)*. It was not until 1835 that the East India Company regulated the production and circulation of coins (no other coins or tokens were to be recognized) at standard weights and wedded the rupee solely to the silver standard.[43] Although control of this monetary system was tightened in 1861, many merchants continued to rely on indigenous credit networks, bills of exchange, and promissory notes, all of which were eventually recognized in the Negotiable Instruments Act of 1881. India joined the gold standard in 1898; the falling price of silver had over decades diminished the value of the rupee, thus disadvantaging Britain's exports and, to the outrage of nationalists, escalating the scale of India's "Home Charges." Ironically, it was only when Britain finally abandoned the gold standard in 1931 that the pound became the genuine basis of an imperial currency system with the creation of the Sterling Area. Even then, Cobden's vision of a world in which Britain's trade flowed freely over distance and national borders unimpeded by competing currency systems remained a chimera.[44]

The creation of standardized weights and measures was equally important in establishing a national and imperial economy as a uniform and neutral space of exchange between strangers. Early modern Europe took its basic unit of weight—the pound—from ancient Rome, but by the sixteenth century local standards ranged as much as 20 percent.[45] In seventeenth century England, there were no less than sixty-four officially sanctioned weights and measures, a tiny fraction of the "tens of thousands of local and regional variations" derived from often elastic standards (a statute defined an inch as the length of three round, dry, barleycorns in 1685) and regulated by several competing jurisdictions.[46] Although the Act of Union attempted to create a unitary British trading standard and taxable unit for Customs and Excise, Scottish weights and measures continued to be used locally for at least another century. Even a single standard like the stannary (100 pounds) had a variety of applications; in Cornish tin mines it amounted to 120 pounds but in the sugar trade it represented 112 pounds, except in the Caribbean, where it was the "short" hundredweight of an even 100 pounds. Different standards of the same unit of measurement were even kept within a few miles of each other: thus in 1754 the standard for the wine gallon held at the Exchequer held 231 cubic inches as opposed to the Guildhall's 224.[47] The culture of scientific experiment, observation, and measurement promoted by the Royal Society heightened interest in developing more precise standards that were transferable across space with new instruments and techniques, but to little effect.

The reform of this chaotic system by centralized standards that were enforced by new instruments that were transferable across space was a protracted affair. A succession of parliamentary enquiries in 1750, 1790, 1814, 1816, and 1820 finally culminated in the Imperial Weights and Measures Act of 1824. This act reduced the units of measurement to just three (the yard, pound, and gallon) and ensured a single standard policed by a new inspectorate whose powers were repeatedly extended in 1835, 1847, 1855, 1858, and 1878.[48] By 1878, when the Board of Trade had sole jurisdiction for the regulation of weights, measures, *and* coins, it controlled an inspectorate empowered to enter any premise or examine the equipment of anyone, anywhere, selling goods. Once again the state had engineered a uniform and abstract national space of exchange in which the problem of trust between strangers was relocated to standardized instruments and practices. Instead of trusting a vendor not to leave you short, you trusted that their scales had been inspected and calibrated on a national standard.

The imperial system was designed to be just that, and though it was adopted across the British Empire, by the end of the nineteenth century its application was uneven. India was made to adopt imperial weights and measures in 1870, but with little effect on its locally and regionally diverse systems with their elastic standards (often based upon the body parts of humans and animals) until the twentieth century. The imperial system did, however, provide common standards for the transcolonial trade that flourished even as international protection grew after the 1870s, as well as for the development of comparable trade statistics across the empire. Here it was in direct competition with the metric system, first adopted by revolutionary France (if momentarily abandoned by Napoleon) and gradually adopted by a further forty-six countries by 1900, including by newly unified nations like Germany and Italy. Although Britain rejected the calls for international standardization around metrification from the 1870s, the realities of international trade meant that the metric system was taught in British schools from 1891.[49] Nonetheless, by the 1920s, 22 percent of the world's population used the British imperial system, including the United States, which had explored the possibility of breaking free of its colonial history by embracing Jefferson's decimal system in the 1790s.

The forging of a uniform national and imperial economy was also made possible by new forms of economic knowledge and calculation. Many of these were again pioneered by the nation-state as it sought to measure and understand the rhythms of the economy so as to render it amenable to government. Again the origins of this process lay in the long eighteenth century between William Petty's attempts to calculate national income in the 1690s and William Playfair's statistical charts and graphs of trade a century later. This work was constrained by the paucity of government records.[50] Established in 1696, the Board of Trade collected data only fitfully in response to specific events or policy questions until the late eighteenth century, when it was still assessing the value of imports and exports at 1696 prices. Thus, although the concepts of national income, balance of trade, and money supply had long existed, they were resignified in the late nineteenth century as new indexes for prices, production, and employment created new ways of mapping the national economy.[51] When unemployment became a statistical category for the first time in 1909 and 1911 (with the introduction of the labor exchange and national insurance), it was accompanied by a new recognition that being unemployed was not a personal moral failure but an economic phenomenon generated by the laws of demand and supply of labor. Similarly, after the Great War, increasingly sophisticated measures of production meant that national income calculations were plotted against estimates of national product and expenditure rather than by wealth through taxation records. This made it possible to picture the national economy, in statistical terms, "as a self-contained 'circular flow' of production, income and expenditure."[52] Mitchell's argument, that the imperial and global nature of the British economy meant it was impossible to imagine it as a manageable national space until the economic crisis of 1929–31 provoked Keynes's *General Theory* (1936), is suggestive but overdrawn.[53] An understanding of the national economy as an abstract and uniform space was a product of the late nineteenth century and was consolidated during the Great War.

Catalyzed by arguments about the cost of war and reparations as well as rising inflation and unemployment, the production of economic statistics accelerated after the Great War and increasingly promoted international comparisons.[54] Whereas trade figures existed for thirty-three countries by 1913, it was possible to statistically map trade between ninety countries by the 1920s; similarly, price indices were published in just two countries in 1903 as opposed to thirty by 1927. Yet the big question, especially in the context of the global economic depression between the wars and the plans for reconstruction that developed during the Second World War, was how to create internationally standardized statistics so that the relative performance of national economies could be analyzed. New international organizations like the International Labor Organization, the United Nations Economic and Social Commission, the International Monetary Fund (IMF), and the Organisation for European Economic Co-operation were critical to this endeavor. Thus, it was not until 1952 that the United Nations standardized national income calculation as gross domestic product, no doubt encouraged by the fact that this was the index that determined national contributions to its funding. In 1939 there were only ten countries that published national income figures; by 1955 the number had risen to seventy-eight. Similarly, the IMF created standardized measures for balance of payment figures in 1948 even though they could only be applied to a small number of countries. Other new types of economic data and forms of calculation—like the percentage of world trade and productivity rates—also developed during the 1940s and 1950s provided fresh points of international comparison and held national governments to account for the relative performance of their economies.[55]

From the 1860s the idea of the economy as an abstract and homogeneous space also owed much to the emergent discipline of economics that studied the laws of its operation. Despite earlier discussions of specific forms of economic activity, the term *political economy* did not arrive until 1767. While chairs of political economy were created in Scotland and London's University College in the early nineteenth century, it became a required subject for civil service exams in 1871, and a few years later Walter Bagehot declared it had become "the common sense of the nation."[56] Its leading early practitioners like Malthus, Ricardo, McCulloch, Martineau, and the two Millses portrayed economic life as inextricable from broader social and political debates. Yet the century that began with the publication of David Ricardo's *On the Principles of Political Economy and Taxation* (1817) closed with Alfred Marshall's

Principles of Economics (1890). The founding fathers of economics—as opposed to political economy—William Jevons and Marshall, bequeathed the discipline a set of questions and an increasingly technical set of skills and specialized terms that were disseminated through new professional forums, such as the *Quarterly Journal of Economics* (1886) and *Economic Journal* (1890) as well as the Royal Economic Society (1890), and slowly institutionalized in universities in the early twentieth century. The new academic discipline pushed hard for the development of better national economic statistics so that its expertise could be better applied to the government of the economy. The production of the economy as a separate domain of expert knowledge and its statistical mapping were mutually reinforcing. By the middle of the twentieth century, the idea of the economy as an abstract, autonomous, and uniform domain had become a natural part of the order of things.[57]

REEMBEDDING

We would be mistaken to assume that even at the turn of the twentieth century economic life was solely characterized by impersonal transactions between strangers and an understanding of the economy as an abstract and homogenous domain. Certainly, as we have seen, the abstraction of economic relations by print culture and new standardized forms of inscription was gradual and uneven: its origins lay in the late seventeenth century, it was evident by the end of the eighteenth century, and it had been naturalized a century later. Yet as this new economy of strangers took root it engendered attempts to reembed economic relations in local and personal knowledge and connections. The new forms of this economy of strangers were matched by equally new practices rooted in local and personal knowledge and connections. This was the dialectic of modernity. I briefly highlight just three: the configuration of the accelerating national and international flows of capital around personal and provincial networks in the stock market; the reinvention of credit relations alongside the cash nexus for an economy of strangers; and the invention of a highly personalized "paternalist" style of management in the new mills and factories of the textile industry.

Financial markets were at the forefront of the invention of impersonal capitalism. They facilitated flows of capital that occurred at increasing speeds over greater distances. Technology was important here. First the telegraph enabled exchanges across and beyond Britain to be networked. Glasgow was the last provincial exchange to join the national network in 1847. London was connected to Paris in 1851, and by 1866 the permanent transatlantic cable reduced the previous sixteen-day relay in price information with New York to twenty minutes, and by 1914 just thirty seconds. As costs tumbled and speeds accelerated, the international flow of telegraphs between stock markets became a veritable flood. By 1909 a telegram left the London Stock Exchange for Europe every second of the working day at 3 percent of the initial cost of transmission in 1851. Similarly, there was a telegram to New York every six seconds at 0.5 percent of the cost in 1866. Such was the impact of the telegraph's collapse of time and distance that London's Stock Exchange extended its hours of business by four hours, until 8 P.M., to facilitate trade with New York. The introduction of the ticker-tape machine in 1872 allowed price information to be removed from the verbal and visual exchanges on the floor and conveyed continuously and simultaneously to anyone, anywhere in the world, who had a receiver. And finally, in 1880, came the telephone. Three years later a separate telephone room was established on the floor of London's Stock Exchange to ease communication between brokers and their offices, who were in turn in touch with investors (some even installed personal lines for their most important clients). By 1908 telephones were ringing every five seconds during the working day with more than eight thousand outward and twenty-four thousand inward calls made. These communication networks helped make London's stock market the financial nerve center of the world, and accordingly its members grew from 363 in 1802 to 906 in 1851 and 5,567 in 1905.[58]

Although by 1900 its stock prices were disseminated in real time across the world, London's exchange and its provincial satellites were exclusive clubs in which personal relations and reputations were key. Transactions on the floor were conducted orally by a code of honor, and brokers who defaulted were named and shamed on a blackboard. Only in the early twentieth century were oral orders made legally binding and paper ledgers required of all transactions. Moral character and personal connections—primarily through family and (private) school—remained essential for admission. As the scale of capital investment grew, so did the importance of partnerships, and because their liabilities remained unlimited, all could be ruined by the actions of a single partner. Because reputations and fortunes rested on the behavior of others, trust and close personal relationships were critical. The same was true in the provincial stock markets that proliferated during the nineteenth century, starting with Dublin in 1799 but accelerating after the formation of the Manchester and Liverpool exchanges in 1836 and ending with Nottingham in 1909. Provincial stock markets provided local investors the chance to trade with local brokers they could meet and the opportunity to invest in local companies they were familiar with. The proliferation of provincial exchanges and the increase in the volume of their trade during the late nineteenth century demonstrated these local connections and knowledge remained important even after the arrival of the telegraph and telephone made it possible to trade on the London Stock Market (where most provincial stock were listed) with up-to-date information on prices from anywhere.[59] In many ways Joel Mokyr's assertion that capital markets "were still based on personal relationships and reputations" in 1800 was equally true a century later.[60]

The impersonal cash economy that had been established and secured during the nineteenth century did not displace the circulation of credit, which remained ubiquitous up to the First World War.[61] Large department stores and cooperatives had flourished from the 1870s, promising to democratize retail relations by dealing only with cash, not credit and reputation, and yet quickly found they had to offer credit to their customers to remain competitive (as 75 percent of cooperatives did by 1900). Department stores and cooperatives accounted for just a tenth of the retail sector by 1915, so its growth was fueled by small, independent shops trading in both cash and credit. The projection of respectability and a reputation for paying one's debts was essential for the acquisition of credit across the social scale. The success or failure of retailers often rested upon their wisdom in deciding whom to extend or refuse credit to.[62]

If local and personal knowledge of customers was essential for commercial survival, it was increasingly hard to maintain in a society of strangers. Trade protection societies thus emerged in the early nineteenth century out of the new urban environments where the prevalence of strangers left retailers most vulnerable when extending credit. Offering information about potential swindlers gleaned from debtor's courts, trade circulars, newspaper reports, and their own agents, they provided "protection" for a broad swathe of local retailers and tradesmen as well as assistance in pursuing debtors through the courts. Recognizing that mobility and anonymity were key attributes of the swindler, the National Association of Trade Protection Societies was formed in 1866 to disseminate information across the country. Even after 1885, when this information was codified into general categories as proto-credit ratings that could be circulated by telegraph, it remained imprecise and dependent upon highly subjective readings of personal appearance and character. However, local trade protection societies continued to thrive, providing indispensable local detail to the national picture and increasingly offering debt collection services by their own salaried (and commissioned) agents. These systems never matched the sophistication of credit rating agencies in the United States. The sheer size of the United States demanded more mobile technologies and standardized forms of credit assessment that in Britain remained shaped by conceptions of character and orientated around the procedures for retrieving rather than preventing debt.[63]

Like the cash nexus, we think of the factory as the very sign of economic modernity. It provided a centralized site of production, the mechanization and functional division of labor, and a new work and time discipline. In short, according to its early nineteenth-century critics, the factory dehumanized workers as interchangeable and transferable components of a new system of production—this "factory system" even reduced women and children to mere units of aggregate labor.[64] The textile districts of Lancashire and Yorkshire were the ground zero of this factory system, and there, in the second half of the nineteenth century, the size of the average spinning and weaving firms increased from 108 to 165 and from 100 to 188 respectively, with the combines expanding from 310 to 429. The concentration of ownership and production, accelerated by the cotton famine in the 1860s, was considerably greater in some places like Preston, where nine firms employed more than a thousand people across sixteen mills. As mills grew in size, owners, who had once worked alongside their employees, became more distant figures relying upon works managers to oversee daily operations.

This distance demanded the cultivation of new bonds of personal loyalty between employer and employees. Some employers, like Stanley Baldwin's mythologized father, boasted they knew the name of every employee and conspicuously displayed this familiarity—in tours of the shop floor, dinners or teas for managers and supervisors, inquiries about the health of a family member, the sending of personally signed birthday cards, and even the presentation of gifts to old hands. It became routine for large employers to project their own family histories upon their workers, providing days off to celebrate the birthdays, comings of age, and weddings of their children or to mourn a death in the family. As businesses were passed from father to son, the cultivation of this broader corporate loyalty to the family was every bit as important as generating a cult of personality around the employer. Not all owners cultivated such personal familiarity; some preferred to develop reputations as successful employers by remaining aloof and retreating to rural estates.[65] Although it was not unknown for workers to be invited to

these estates on special occasions, their distance and grandeur was supposed to generate awe and wonder, not familiarity. As work managers
became increasingly common, the owners' presence was manifested by,
say, the support of a factory band or football team, the construction of
workers' houses or recreation facilities. Freed from an intimate knowledge of their businesses, factory owners cultivated their personal
authority and reputations by becoming local notables, patronizing the
broader community with libraries, parks, and Sunday schools, or serving as magistrates, poor law guardians or even MPs. The point is that
when factories and firms grew to a size at which it was no longer viable
for employers to know or daily encounter their workers, they invented
different techniques to project their personal authority and reputations
upon a supposedly impersonal and dehumanizing form of production.

· · ·

Britons inhabited a new type of economy by the late nineteenth century: one that had adapted around the society of strangers. Markets that
had once been structured around local and face-to-face interactions
were remade as abstract spaces with impersonal forms of exchange that
made it possible to do business with strangers. At the heart of this transition lay the ability of print culture to abstract information from person and place and disseminate it across distance. Yet the state also
helped forge a new conception of the economy as a uniform and homogenous domain, one bound together by the standardization of money
and weights and measures. Once the state had guaranteed the uniformity of these forms of inscription, the problem of knowing *whom* to trust
that had long plagued economic relations was largely resolved by
instead knowing *what* to trust. If print culture helped markets extend
beyond the local and even to imagine an economy of strangers, the
state provided the infrastructure that made it possible to conceive of
the economy as a homogenous national and imperial space. This process may have been gradual and uneven—stretching the late seventeenth century through to the early twentieth century—but we might

take *The Economist* under Bagehot's editorship as marking a key moment of its arrival. It was also a dialectical process, because this great transformation was so fraught that it generated attempts to manage the economy of strangers by reembedding it in local and personal relations.

Conclusion

Nearly everyone can agree that over the past three centuries the world has been made modern. The speed and scale of that great transformation was unprecedented in the history of the human race. Indeed, one frequently noted characteristic of we moderns is our consciousness that the world around us is always changing, that we face an open-ended future to be thought and made anew. Perhaps this is one reason why it has become almost impossible to find agreement about what it is that characterizes modern life, or where and when those characteristics were first apparent. There are many reasons for this, but arguably the chief one has been the revolt against theories of modernization that mapped the historical development of the world in a linear sequence according to an (often inaccurate) understanding of Euro-American experience. Because it is now seemingly impossible to define the condition of modernity, or to locate its origins, historians have either grown wary of trying to do so or strangely promiscuous in identifying the modern almost everywhere. Such has been the resulting confusion that some have just suggested dispensing with the term *modernity* as a useful analytical category. And yet it remains hard-wired into the very temporal structure of the discipline of history (the ancient, medieval, early modern, and modern), and historians (and others) still routinely use it all the time in the classes they teach and the books they write, because without the term it is difficult to think comparatively about historical change over time and across space. And, at the end of the day, that is the job of the historian. The purpose of this book, then, has been to rehabilitate modernity as an analytical category for historians so that we can do that work.

To do so I have developed an understanding of modernity that is both historically and culturally specific. Using Britain as a case study, so often the testing ground for theories of modernization, I have argued that Britain was not made modern by possessive Protestant individuals, the revolution of 1688, the Enlightenment, or the Industrial Revolution. Instead, the sustained and rapid growth of a population that was increasingly concentrated in urban areas and mobile over ever-greater distances within and beyond the nation created a new and distinctly modern society of strangers. Living among strangers posed considerable and unprecedented challenges to the organization of social, political, and economic life that had long predominantly but not exclusively cohered around local and personal relations. Whereas forms of sociability, authority, association, and exchange had once primarily relied upon face-to-face encounters in specific places, these were slowly undermined by the growing size, anonymity, and mobility of the population. As a series of new and very different social, political, and economic problems developed, the emergent nation-state, together with a range of people animated by varied motivations, increasingly deployed systems of abstraction to comprehend these changes and reengineer society, polity, and economy so that they could operate in a society of strangers and over the vast distances of the empire. Because these new abstract systems of thought and organization were transferable across space, they addressed distant strangers in uniform and impersonal ways. Yet, because they were not always effective, and even when they were, many failed to trust or were alienated from them, they also generated fresh attempts to reembed economic, social, and political relations in person and place. The dialectic of abstraction and the reinvention of local and personal relations was how we moderns navigated the numerous challenges generated by living in a society of strangers who moved over ever-greater distances.

Let me reiterate that this does not mean that those who were not modern—those once characterized by anthropologists and sociologists as "traditional"—did not experience profound changes. The transitions among the ancient, medieval, and early modern worlds were clearly epochal. Nor am I suggesting that earlier societies did not deal with rapid population growth, mobility, urbanization, encounters with strangers, and expanding empires. It would clearly be an absurd caricature to suggest that before the modern era people lived only in small communities where they knew everyone. Abstract and impersonal systems of organization were also not unique to the modern world; they had had a long germination in the early modern worlds of Asia and Europe. The radical novelty of the modern world was the unprecedented scale of these phenomena.

And this scale was first evident in Britain. Britons were the first to inhabit a society of strangers, because Britain was the first to break the Malthusian trap and sustain rapid population growth, the first to become a predominantly urban society, the first to create systems of transportation and communication that allowed people and information to travel over greater distances at increasing speeds. The scale of this transformation required not just a reconfiguration of social, political, and economic relations, but new ways of governing them that led to an unprecedentedly extensive application of systems of abstract thought and organization. The claim that Britons were probably the first moderns is not a value judgment. It is not an attempt to valorize Britain's historical experience as a world historical model that all others have to follow. Nor is there any wistful nostalgia for how Britain was made Great by the supposed genius of its people for invention, exploration, tolerance, and stability. Just as there was no master race, so there was no master plan that ensured an inexorable forward march to modernity. Britain's modernity was the product of a highly contingent and experimental process; it was the consequence of contingent responses to diverse problems.

Britain became modern only in the nineteenth century; it was then that the scale of the great transformation was evident. I am not beguiled by the attempts either to locate Britain's modernity in the seventeenth or eighteenth centuries or to insist that it was placed on hold until the twentieth century by the stubborn grip of Britain's *ancien regime*. Time and again we have seen how processes that may have been seeded in the late seventeenth century sprouted during the mid-eighteenth century and came to bloom between the 1830s and the 1880s, even if some did not reach fruition until the early twentieth century. It was only in the nineteenth century that the full nature of the society of strangers, the increasing reach and speed of new technologies of transportation and communication, and the grip of abstract and impersonal systems of social, political, and economic organization became apparent.

Without question Britain's increasingly massive empire helped shape its experience of modernity, but it was not the catalyst of it. This helps qualify the new orthodoxy that British, and indeed European history generally, was written overseas and actively constituted by the imperial encounter. Because the force of this argument is often lessened by its indiscriminate application, it is important to emphasize that, even though growing numbers of Britons emigrated to imperial territories, the formation of a society of strangers in Britain had little to do with its empire. And yet the forging of an imperial polity and economy was hugely influential in the development of new abstract and impersonal forms of government and exchange. Governing distant agents, populations, and colonial officials did often generate the invention or development new systems of abstraction and bureaucratic management. And certainly the expanding grid of a transport and communications infrastructure shrank the British world and made possible new forms of exchange, government, and association between distant strangers. And yet, it was frequently the case that those systems were exported from Britain and failed to take root in colonial settings—think of how late and inaccurately many colonial censuses were instantiated and what an utter failure the imperial census was. Moreover, the limits of those systems, or the sense that they were less effective upon "traditional" peoples, also ensured that local and personal forms of authority and "indirect" rule proliferated in the dialectic of colonial modernity. Empire may have helped shape the experience of Britain's modernity, but it was certainly not always already determinative of it.

If empire did not do it, what did usher in the modern era in Britain? As modernization theory was plagued by the quest for a single origin or cause that could explain the great transformation, I have purposively sidestepped the question of causation, focusing instead on how, not why, Britain became modern. As I have repeatedly made clear, the condition of modernity was not just the advent of a society of strangers but the techniques of abstraction and embedding with which it was managed. Nonetheless, at this point some readers will have grown tired of my emphasis on the contingencies of this process and will no doubt accuse me of failing to explain what caused the exogenous population growth that was so critical to the creation of a society of strangers. So let me be clear: I do not believe there is a single explanation (let alone one that is transferable to other places) of either why Britain broke through the Malthusian trap and sustained demographic growth or rapidly urbanized. Even though the neo-Malthusian orthodoxy currently argue that effectively rising wages enabled people to marry younger and have more children, there remains an abundant literature that points to the importance of new conceptions of childhood and marriage, the improvement of agricultural productivity, and the development of public health infrastructures. Similarly, the increasing mobility and urbanization of the population was not simply the product of the quest for work produced by industrialization, important as that was. We have seen that the emergent nation-state often drove improvements in transportation and that marriage, religion, politics, education, and much else kept people on the move. Nor does it make sense to explain the society of strangers and the dialectic of abstraction and reembedding it unleashed as the work of liberalism broadly conceived. In other words, the condition of modernity does not have to be explained solely by reference to the economic, political, and cultural changes generally associated with the Industrial Revolution and the Enlightenment, although elements of both played their parts. We do not need a singular cause of modernity for that category to be analytically useful.

If I have been able to use the British case to rehabilitate a history of modernity, what, we may finally ask, is the payoff for historians of other parts of the world? It is certainly not a question of taking sides and being for or against modernity. Although in Britain there came to be a normative basis to how the realms of society, polity, and economy were conceived and organized, these were not necessarily intrinsic to the dialectic of modernity. To assume so would be deeply depressing, for it would evacuate the work of politics and human agency—our ability to think and organize the world differently even while acknowledging that that work would always depend upon forms of abstraction and reembedding. If there is a politics to rehabilitating modernity as a useful analytical category, it is to allow historians to make sense of broad and generally shared patterns of historical change so that we can think comparatively across time and space. I hope that by returning to the macro-questions that shaped our discipline we can recapture its explanatory ambitions from the navel-gazing of microhistories and in the process reestablish an understanding of the public utility of our work.

Although the comparative treatment in this book is insufficient, it seeks to invite others to test its arguments elsewhere. Clearly, as we began to see in chapter 1, other countries followed Britain in breaking through the Malthusian trap and, by the twentieth century especially, often came to exceed its rates of population growth, urbanization, and mobility. It is my conjecture that if this signaled a shared historical process, it was one with alternative trajectories and iterations, for like Britain every society has its own unique path to sustained population growth and mobility. A product of contingent circumstances, the speed, scale, and intensity of this process varied enormously from country to country. Nonetheless, once a society of strangers had taken shape, it generated similar problems of remaking the forms of government, exchange, and association that were in turn addressed by culturally specific forms of abstraction and embedding. My argument is modular; it is not monocausal or diffusionist. The holy grail of modernization theory—a single origin for a singular modernity that all should progress to—does not exist; in each local setting it manifested and was experienced in its own peculiar ways. If that is the case, we might be able to write a history of global modernity that is plural in cause and singular in condition. We might, in short, have finally laid the ghost of modernization theory to rest.

NOTES

I. WHAT IS MODERNITY?

1. Karl Marx and Friedrich Engels, *The Communist Manifesto* (London: Penguin, [1888] 2002), 223.

2. Karl Polanyi, *The Great Transformation* (Boston: Beacon Press, [1944] 2001).

3. Walt Whitman Rostow, *The Stages of Economic Growth: A Non-Communist Manifesto* (Cambridge: Cambridge University Press, 1960).

4. Émile Durkheim, *The Elementary Forms of Religious Life* (New York: Free Press [1915] 1965); Mustafa Emirbayer (ed.), *Emile Durkheim: Sociologist of Modernity* (Oxford: Blackwell, 2003); Georg Simmel, *The Sociology of Georg Simmel* (New York: Free Press, 1950); *On Individuality and Its Social Forms* (Chicago: University of Chicago Press, 1972).

5. Ferdinand Tonnies, *Community and Society* (Cambridge: Cambridge University Press, [1887] 2001).

6. Bernard Yack, *The Fetishism of Modernities: Epochal Self-Consciousness in Contemporary Social and Political Thought* (Notre Dame, IN: University of Notre Dame Press, 1997).

7. On modernization theory generally, M. Latham, *Modernization as Ideology: American Social Science and "Nation Building" in the Kennedy Era* (Chapel Hill: University of North Carolina Press, 2000); N. Gilman, *Mandarins of the Future: Modernization Theory in Cold War America* (Baltimore: Johns Hopkins University Press, 2003); and on Britain see J. Hodge, *Triumph of the Expert: Agrarian Doctrines of Development and the Legacies of British Colonialism* (Athens: Ohio University Press, 2007).

8. Eric Williams, *Capitalism and Slavery* (Chapel Hill: University of North Carolina Press, [1944] 1994); Edward Said, *Orientalism* (New York: Vintage, [1978] 1994).

9. Frederick Cooper, *Colonialism in Question: Theory, Knowledge, History* (Berkeley: University of California Press, 2005), 7.

10. Among many, see D. Chakrabarty, *Habitations of Modernity* (Chicago: University of Chicago Press, 2002); T. Mitchell, *Questions of Modernity* (Minneapolis: University of Minnesota Press, 2000); A. Appadurai, *Modernity at Large* (Minneapolis: University of Minnesota Press, 1996); S. Eisenstadt, "Multiple Modernities," *Daedalus,*129, 1 (2000), 1–29.

11. Cooper, *Colonialism in Question*, ch. 5. In the British context see B. Rieger and M. Daunton (eds.), *Meanings of Modernity: Britain from the Late Victorian Era to World War Two* (London: Berg, 2001); M. Nava and A. O'Shea (eds.), *Modern Times: Reflections on a Century of English Modernity* (Abingdon, UK: Routledge, 1996); Kathleen Wilson, *The New Imperial History: Culture, Identity and Modernity in Britain and Empire, 1660–1840* (Cambridge: Cambridge University Press, 2004).

12. A. Light, *Forever England: Feminity, Literature and Conservatism between the Wars* (Abingdon, UK: Routledge, 1991); A. Burton (ed.), *Gender, Sexuality and Colonial Modernities* (Abingdon, UK: Routledge, 1999); L. Doan and J. Garrity (eds.), *Sapphic Modernities: Sexuality, Women and National Culture* (Houndmills, UK: Palgrave Macmillan, 2004); D. Gilbert, D. Matless, and B. Short (eds.), *Geographies of British Modernity* (Oxford: Blackwell, 2003); P. Tinkler and C. Krasnick Warsh, "Feminine Modernity in Interwar Britain and North America," *Journal of Women's History*, 20, 3 (2008), 113–43.

13. Cooper, *Colonialism in Question*; "AHR Roundtable: Historians and the Question of 'Modernity,'" *American Historical Review*, 116, 3 (2011), 631–751.

14. Max Weber, *The Protestant Ethic and the Spirit of Capitalism* (London: Allen and Unwin, [1905] 1930); R. H. Tawney, *Religion and the Rise of Capitalism* (London: Pelican, 1926).

15. Kenneth Pomeranz, *The Great Divergence: China, Europe, and the Making of the Modern World Economy* (Princeton, NJ: Princeton University Press, 2001).

16. Thanks largely to the legacies of modernization theory, there are already answers to this question and many that assert that Britain was the first to become modern. For examples, see, P. Mathias, *The First Industrial Nation: An Economic History of Britain 1700–1914* (London: Methuen, 1969); H. Perkin, *The Origins of Modern English Society, 1780–1880* (London: Routledge, 1969); A. L. Beier et al. (eds.), *The First Modern Society* (Cambridge: Cambridge University Press, 1989); R. Porter, *The Creation of the Modern World* (New York: Norton,

2001); D. Wahrman, *The Making of the Modern Self* (New Haven: Yale University Press, 2004); Steve Pincus, *1688: The First Modern Revolution* (New Haven: Yale University Press, 2009).

17. Georg Simmel, "The Stranger," in *On Individuality and Social Forms* (Chicago: University of Chicago Press, 1971), 143–49.

18. Massimo Livi Bacci, *The Population of Europe. A History* (Oxford: Blackwell, 2000).

19. Roger Schofield, "British Population Change, 1700–1871," in Roderick Floud and Paul Johnson (eds.), *The Economic History of Britain since 1700*, vol. 1 (Cambridge: Cambridge University Press, 1994), 60–95; Michael Anderson, "The Social Implications of Demographic Change," in F.M.L. Thompson (ed.), *The Cambridge Social History of Britain*, vol. 2 (Cambridge: Cambridge University Press, 1993), 1–71; R. Schofield and E.A. Wrigley, *Population and Economy: Population and History from the Traditional to the Modern World* (Cambridge: Cambridge University Press, 1986).

20. Figures for compounded annual rates of growth from Massimo Livi-Bacci, *A Concise History of World Population* (Oxford: Blackwell, 2007) are broken down as follows:

	Asia	Europe	USSR	Africa	America	Oceana	World
0–1750	.06	.07	.06	.08	.02	.06	.06
1750–1950	.51	.63	.82	.38	1.46	.74	.59
1950–	1.9	.53	.97	2.51	1.83	1.67	1.75

21. I am here using the metric of the urban as 10,000 inhabitants to help capture the *intensive* experience of urbanization in the modern period, when large cities get larger and the predominant urban experience is to live in big cities. The early modern experience, in comparison, is of *extensive* urbanization, when there are many smaller conurbations that get defined as urban with between 2,500 and 10,000 inhabitants. Thanks to Trevor Jackson for this distinction. Jan de Vries, *European Urbanization* (Cambridge, MA: Harvard University Press, 1984).

22. Figures from B.R. Mitchell, *International Historical Statistics. Europe 1750–2005* (Basingstoke, UK: Palgrave Macmillan, 2007); idem, *International Historical Statistics. Africa, Asia and Oceania, 1750–2005* (Basingstoke, UK: Palgrave Macmillan, 2007); idem, *International Historical Statistics. The Americas, 1750–2005* (Basingstoke, UK: Palgrave Macmillan, 2007).

23. These figures, drawn from the United Nations, Economic and Social Affairs, *World Urbanization Prospects. The 2005 Revision* (New York: United

Nations, 2006), should be viewed skeptically, because the United Nations uses a "floating" standard of urbanization, that is, it uses whatever standard national governments take!

24. E. Salmon and J. Worsfold (eds.), *British Dominions Year Book 1918* (London: Eagle, Star and British Dominions Insurance Co, 1918).

25. Jules Verne, *Around the World in Eighty Days* (London: Sampson, Low, Marston and Searle, 1873); John Seeley, *The Expansion of England* (Cambridge: Cambridge University Press, 1883), 296.

26. James Belich, *Replenishing the Earth: The Settler Revolution and the Rise of the Anglo-World, 1783–1939* (Oxford: Oxford University Press, 2009), 4.

27. Christopher Bayly, *The Birth of the Modern World, 1780–1914* (Oxford: Blackwell, 2009), ch. 3.

28. Suggestive exceptions are Lloyd and Susanne Rudolph, *The Modernity of Tradition: Political Development in India* (Chicago: University of Chicago Press, 1967); Eric Hobsbawm and Terence Ranger (eds.), *The Invention of Tradition* (Cambridge: Cambridge University Press, 1983).

29. A strong case has been made for the 1880s as the decisive moment when Britain became modern, but this underestimates the accelerating pace of change from the 1830s. Jose Harris, *Private Lives, Public Spirit: Britain 1870–1914* (London: Penguin, 1993); Richard Price, *British Society 1680–1880: Dynamism, Containment and Change* (Cambridge: Cambridge University Press, 1999).

2. A SOCIETY OF STRANGERS

1. In a very long debate see, most recently, Charles H. Feinstein, "Pessimism Perpetuated: Real Wages and the Standard of Living in Britain during and after the Industrial Revolution," *Journal of Economic History,* 58, 3 (1998), 625–58; Emma Griffin, *A Short History of the British Industrial Revolution* (New York: Palgrave Macmillan, 2010), ch. 9.

2. Simon Szreter, *Fertility, Class and Gender in Britain 1860–1940* (Cambridge: Cambridge University Press, 1996); Massimo Livi Bacci, *A Concise History of World Population* (Oxford: Blackwell, 2007), ch. 4.

3. Norma Landau, "The Regulation of Immigration, Economic Structures and Definitions of the Poor in Eighteenth Century England," *Historical Journal,* 33, 3 (1990), 541–72; Peter Clark and David Souden (eds.), *Migration and Society in Early Modern England* (London: Rowman and Littlefield, 1988). Leslie Page Moloch, *Moving Europeans: Migration in Western Europe Since 1650* (Bloomington: Indiana University Press, 2003).

4. Joel Mokyr, *The Enlightened Economy: An Economic History of Britain 1700–1850* (New Haven: Yale University Press, 2010), 305.

5. The figures are, respectively, 55.9, 54.6, and 40.9 as opposed to 38.3. Colin G. Pooley and Jean Turnbull, *Migration and Mobility in Britain since the Eighteenth Century* (London: UCL Press, 1998), 3.

6. A recent study of more than 16,000 life histories has shown that between the 1750s and the 1920s the mean distance of migration remained remarkably short at less than twenty-five miles. Pooley and Turnbull, *Migration and Mobility*, ch. 3.

7. Richard Dennis, "Modern London," in Martin Daunton (ed.), *Cambridge Urban History of Britain, Vol. III, 1840–1950* (Cambridge: Cambridge University Press), 117.

8. Michael Anderson, "The Social Implications of Demographic Change," in F.M.L.Thompson (ed.), The *Cambridge Social History of Britain, 1750–1950. Vol. 2, People and their Environment* (Cambridge: Cambridge University Press, 1990), 11–13.

9. Lynn Hollen Lees and Paul Hohenberg, *The Making of Urban Europe, 1000–1994* (Cambridge, MA: Harvard University Press, 1995).

10. With only seventy towns with more than 2,500 inhabitants and only three cities with populations over 20,000, technically in 1700 just "1% of the population ... fell within the modern demographic measure of urbanism." Peter Borsay, *The English Urban Renaissance: Culture and Society in the Provincial Town* (Oxford: Oxford University Press, 1991), 3.

11. F.M.L. Thompson, "Town and City," in F.M.L. Thompson (ed.), *The Cambridge Social History of Britain, 1750–1950, Vol. 1, Regions and Communities* (Cambridge: Cambridge University Press, 1990), 13–14.

12. Arthur Redford, *Labour Migration in England, 1800–1850* (Manchester: Manchester University Press, [1926] 1976), ch. 9.

13. Nor should we forget the 150,000 children who were sent to Britain's white settler colonies from prisons, workhouses, or orphanages by a range of voluntary societies. Although the vast majority of 90,000 were sent between the 1870s and the 1920s, such schemes continued to operate as late as 1967. Ronald Findlay and Kevin H. O'Rourke, *Power and Plenty: Trade, War, and the World Economy in the Second Millennium* (Princeton, NJ: Princeton University Press, 2009), 231; R. Lawton, "Population and Society 1730–1914," in R.A. Dogshon and R.A. Butlin (eds.), *An Historical Geography of England and Wales* (London: Academic Press, 1990), 288–90; Marjory Harper and Stephen Constantine, *Migration and Empire* (Oxford: Oxford University Press, 2010).

14. Kenneth Morgan, *Slavery, Atlantic Trade and the British Economy, 1660–1800* (Cambridge: Cambridge University Press, 2001), 10.

15. David Northrup, *Indentured Labor in the Age of Imperialism, 1834–1922* (Cambridge: Cambridge University Press, 2005).

16. These paragraphs rely on Joanna Guldi, *Roads to Power: Britain Invents the Infrastructure State* (Cambridge, MA: Harvard University Press, 2012).

17. Arthur Redford, *Labour Migration in England, 1800–1850* (Manchester: Manchester University Press, [1926] 1964), 189.

18. Daniel R. Headrick, *The Tools of Empire: Technology and European Imperialism in the Nineteenth Century* (New York: Oxford University Press, 1981), pt. III.

19. Anne D. Wallace, *Walking, Literature, and English Culture: The Origins and Uses of Peripatetic in the Nineteenth Century* (Oxford: Clarendon Press, 1993); James Sharpe, *Dick Turpin: The Myth of the English Highwayman* (London: Profile Books, 2004); Kim A. Wagner, *Thuggee: Banditry and the British in Early Nineteenth Century India* (Cambridge: Cambridge University Press, 2007).

20. Richard Gooch, "A Few Thoughts on Small-Talk," *New Monthly Magazine 5* (January–June 1823), 217. Quoted in Jo Guldi, *Roads to Power: Britain Invents the Infrastructure State* (Cambridge, MA: Harvard University Press, 2012), 191.

21. Wolfgang Schivelbusch, *The Railway Journey: The Industrialization of Time and Space in the Nineteenth Century* (Berkeley: University of California Press, 1986).

22. Charles Dickens, "Street Sketches No.1," *Morning Chronicle*, September 26, 1834, reprinted in *The Works of Charles Dickens: Sketches by Boz* (New York: P. F. Collier and Son, 1911), 129–30; Charles Manby Smith, *Curiosities of London Life, or Phases, Physiological and Social of the Great Metropolis* (London: W. and F. G. Cash, 1857), 227–33; C. L. E. "London Society Underground," *London Society*, 1, 3 (May 1863), 267–62.

23. Max Schlesinger, *Saunterings in and about London* (London: Nathaniel Cooke, 1853), 155–56. G. F. Cruchley, *Cruchley's London in 1865: A Handbook for Strangers* (London, 1865).

24. Miles Ogborn, *Spaces of Modernity: London's Geographies 1680–1780* (London: Guilford Press, 1998), ch. 4.

25. In Wordsworth's words, "Above all, one thought / Baffled my understanding: how men lived / Even next-door neighbours, as we say, yet still /Strangers, not knowing each the other's name." Book 7, "The Prelude," 115. http://www.gutenberg.org/files/12383/12383-h/Wordsworth3c.html#24b7

26. William Hazlitt, "On Londoners and Country People" (1823) and Thomas de Quincey, "The Nation of London" (1834) both in Rick Allen, *The Mov-*

ing Pageant: A Literary Sourcebook on London Street-Life, 1700–1914 (London: Routledge, 1998), 109–12 and 117–19.

27. Quoted in Harry Cocks, *Nameless Offences: Homosexual Desire in the Nineteenth Century* (London: I.B. Tauris, 2003), 96; Penelope Corfield, "Walking the City Streets: The Urban Odyssey in Eighteenth-Century England," *Journal of Urban History*, 16, 2 (1990), 132–74.

28. Cocks, *Nameless Offences*; Judith Walkowitz, *City of Dreadful Delight: Narratives of Sexual Danger in Late-Victorian London* (London: Virago, 1992); Peter Bailey, *Popular Culture and Performance in the Victorian City* (Cambridge: Cambridge University Press, 1998); Lynda Nead, *Victorian Babylon: People, Streets and Images in Nineteenth Century London* (New Haven: Yale University Press, 2005); Koven, *Slumming: Sexual and Social Politics in Victorian London* (Princeton, NJ: Princeton University Press, 2006).

29. Caroline Arscott, "The Representation of the City in the Visual Arts," in Daunton (ed.), *The Cambridge Urban History of Britain*, 811–32.

30. Lucy Hartley, *Physiognomy and the Meaning of Expression in Nineteenth Century Culture* (Cambridge: Cambridge University Press, 2001); Jonathan Finn, *Capturing the Criminal Image: From Mug Shot to Surveillance Society* (Minneapolis: University of Minnesota Press, 2009).

31. David Cannadine, *The Rise and Fall of Class in Britain* (New York: Columbia University Press, 1999); *Ornamentalism: How the British Saw their Empire* (New York: Oxford University Press, 2001).

32. P. Abrams, *The Origins of British Sociology, 1834–1914* (Chicago: University of Chicago Press, 1968); M. Bulmer, K. Bales, and K.K. Sclar (eds.) *The Social Survey in Historical Perspective, 1880–1940* (Cambridge: Cambridge University Press, 1996); Lawrence Goldman, *Science, Reform and Politics in Victorian Britain: The Social Science Association 1857–1886* (Cambridge: Cambridge University Press, 2002); Mark Freeman, *Social Investigation in Rural England, 1870–1914* (Rochester, NY: Boydell Press, 2003); Thomas Osborne, Nikolas Rose, and Mike Savage, "Reinscribing British Sociology: Some Critical Reflections," *Sociological Review*, 56, 4 (2008), 519–34.

33. Stephen Kern, *The Culture of Time and Space, 1880–1918* (Cambridge, MA: Harvard University Press, 1983); Susanna Barrows, *Distorting Mirrors: Visions of the Crowd in Late Nineteenth Century France* (New Haven: Yale University Press, 1981).

34. P.J. Keating, *Into Unknown England, 1866–1913: Selections from the Social Explorers* (London: Rowman and Littlefield, 1976); John Marriott and Masaie Matsumura (eds.), *The Metropolitan Poor: Semi-Factual Accounts 1795–1910*. 2 vols. (London: Pickering and Chatto, 1999); Koven, *Slumming.*

35. Thomas Metcalf, *Ideologies of the Raj* (Cambridge: Cambridge University Press, 1997); Catherine Hall, *Civilized Subjects: Metropole and Colony in the English Imagination 1830–1867* (Chicago: University of Chicago Press, 2002); Karuna Mantena, *Alibis of Empire: Henry Maine and the Ends of Liberal Imperialism* (Princeton, NJ: Princeton University Press, 2010); Nancy Stepan, *The Idea of Race in Science: Great Britain, 1800–1960* (London; Archon, 1982).

36. Gareth Stedman Jones, *Languages of Class; Studies in English Working Class History, 1832–1982* (Cambridge: Cambridge University Press 1983); Patrick Joyce, *Visions of the People: Industrial England the Question of Class, c. 1848–1914* (Cambridge: Cambridge University Press, 1991); Dror Wahrman, *Imagining the Middle Class: The Political Representation of. Class in Britain, c. 1780–1840* (Cambridge: Cambridge University Press, 1995); Jon Lawrence, *Speaking for the People: Party, Language and Popular Politics in England, 1867–1914* (Cambridge: Cambridge University Press, 1998).

37. Jon Lawrence, "Labour and the Politics of Class, 1900–1940," in D. Feldman and J. Lawrence (eds.), *Structures and Transformations in Modern British History: Essays for Gareth Stedman Jones* (Cambridge: Cambridge University Press, 2011); Mike Savage, *Identities and Social Change in Britain since 1940* (Oxford: Oxford University Press, 2010).

38. Alan MacFarlane, *The Origins of English Individualism: The Family Property and Social Transition* (Oxford: Blackwell, 1978); Lawrence Stone, *Family, Sex and Marriage in England 1500–1800* (New York: Harper and Row, 1977); Leonore Davidoff and Catherine Hall, *Family Fortunes: Men and Women of the English Middle Class 1780–1850* (London: Routledge, 2002); Jan de Vries, *The Industrious Revolution: Consumer Behavior and the Household Economy, 1650 to the Present* (Cambridge: Cambridge University Press, 2008).

39. Anderson, "The Social Implications of Demographic Change," 65.

40. John Gillis, *A World of Their Own Making: Myth, Ritual and the Quest for Family Values* (New York: HarperCollins, 1996).

41. This paragraph owes much to Anderson, "The Social Implications of Demographic Change," 39–46. The exception here was what sociologists and social historians in the 1950s and 1960s regarded as the traditional working-class family form where the extended family lived in the same neighborhood and shared child-raising responsibilities. Yet as the product of the early twentieth century, this type of family was actually of very recent historical vintage, and it disappeared as quickly as it had arrived at the hands of postwar urban planners, the decline of large scale manufacturing industry, and new critiques of the family.

42. Davidoff and Hall, *Family Fortunes*.

43. Gillis, *A World of Their Own Making*.

44. Elizabeth Buettner, *Empire Families: Britons and Late Imperial India* (Oxford: Oxford University Press, 2005).

45. Susan Whyman, *The Pen and the People: English Letter Writers, 1660–1800* (Oxford: Oxford University Press, 2009); David Vincent, *Literacy and Popular Culture: England, 1750–1914* (Cambridge: Cambridge University Press, 1989), ch. 2.

46. Buettner, *Empire Families*; Michael Roper, *The Secret Battle: Emotional Survival in the Great War* (Manchester: Manchester University Press, 2009).

47. Harry Cocks, "The Cost of Marriage and the Matrimonial Agency in Late Victorian Britain," *Social History*, 38, 1 (2013), 66–88.

48. Harry Cocks, *Classified: The Secret History of the Personal Column* (London: Random House, 2009).

49. Charles Taylor, *Sources of the Self: The Making of Modern Identity* (Cambridge, MA: Harvard1992); Carolyn Steedman, *Strange Dislocations: Childhood and the Idea of Human Interiority, 1780–1930* (Cambridge, MA: Harvard University Press, 1995); Roy Porter (ed.), *Rewriting the Self: Histories from the Renaissance to the Present* (London: Routledge, 1996); Dror Wahrman, *The Making of the Modern Self: Identity and Culture in the Eighteenth Century England* (New Haven: Yale University Press, 2006).

50. And therefore not simply as an arena for the transgressive blurring of gender, race, and class. Terry Castle, *Masquerade and Civilization: The Carnivalesque in Eighteenth Century English Fiction and Culture* (Stanford, CA: Stanford University Press, 1986); Wahrman, *The Making of the Modern Self*.

51. Bailey, *Popular Culture and Performance in the Victorian City*; Koven, *Slumming*; James Vernon, "'For Some Queer Reason': The Trials and Tribulations of Colonel Barker," *Signs*, 26, 1 (2000), 37–62; Angus McLaren, "Smoke and Mirrors: Willy Clarkson and the Role of Disguises in Inter War England," *Journal of Social History*, 40, 3 (2007), 597–618.

52. David Anixter, "Born Again for the First Time: Religious Conversion, Self and Society in Britain, c. 1680–1850." PhD diss. University of California-Berkeley, forthcoming, 2015; David Vincent, *Bread, Knowledge: A Study of Nineteenth Century Working Class Autobiography* (London: Routledge, 1982); Brian Harrison, *Drink and the Victorians: The Temperance Question in England 1815–1872* (Keele: Keele University Press, 1971); Stefan Collini, "The Idea of 'Character' in Victorian Political Thought," *Transactions of the Royal Historical Society*, 5th Series, 35 (1985), 29–50.

53. Alison Winter, *Mesmerized: Powers of Mind in Victorian Britain* (Chicago: University of Chicago Press, 1998); Alex Owen, *The Place of Enchantment: British Occultism and the Culture of the Modern* (Chicago: University of Chicago Press, 2004); Nikolas Rose, *Governing the Soul: The Shaping of the Private Self* (London: Routledge, 1999); Mathew Thomson, *Psychological Subjects: Identity, Health and Culture in Twentieth Century Britain* (Oxford: Oxford University Press, 2006).

3. GOVERNING STRANGERS

1. For a small sampling of a voluminous literature, see G. R. Elton, *The Tudor Revolution in Government: Administrative Changes in the Reign of Henry VIII* (Cambridge: Cambridge University Press, 1953); Michael J. Braddick, *State Formation in Early Modern England, 1550–1700* (Cambridge: Cambridge University Press, 2000); John Brewer, *Sinews of Power: War, Money and the English State, 1688–1783* (Cambridge, MA: Harvard University Press, 1989); Lawrence Stone (ed.), *An Imperial State at War: Britain from 1689 to 1815* (London: Routledge, 1994); Oliver MacDonagh, "The Nineteenth Century Revolution in Government," *Historical Journal*, 1 (1958), 52–67; James Cronin, *The Politics of State Expansion: War, State and Society in Twentieth Century Britain* (London: Routledge, 1991).

2. Benjamin Elman, *A Cultural History of Civil Examinations in Late Imperial China* (Berkeley: University of California Press, 2000).

3. Although some of these new forms of statecraft were prefigured by the East India Company's government of South Asia, they were primarily intended, like the civil service exams in imperial China, not to govern strangers but to discipline administrators with bureaucratic routines. Eric Stokes, *The English Utilitarians and India* (Oxford: Oxford University Press, 1990 [1959]); Jon E. Wilson, *The Domination of Strangers: Modern Governance in Eastern India, 1780–1835* (Basingstoke: Palgrave Macmillan, 2008). See also Bhavani Raman, *Document Raj: Writing and Scribes in Early Colonial South India* (Chicago: University of Chicago Press, 2012).

4. Edward Higgs, *The Information State in England: The Central Collection of Information on Citizens, 1500–2000* (Basingstoke: Palgrave Macmillan, 2004); Daniel R. Headrick, *When Information Came of Age: Technologies of Knowledge in the Age of Reason and Revolution 1700–1850* (New York: Oxford University Press, 2002); Mike Braddick, *State Formation in Early Modern England, c. 1550–1700* (Cambridge: Cambridge University Press, 2000).

5. Gabriel Wolfenstein, "Public Numbers and the Victorian State: The General Registrar's Office, the Census, and Statistics in Nineteenth Century

Britain." PhD diss. University of California-Los Angeles, 2004; idem., "Recounting the Nation: The General Register Office and Victorian Bureaucracies," *Centaurus*, 49, 4 (2007), 261–88.

6. Bernard S. Cohn, "The Census, Social Structure and Objectification in South Asia," *An Anthropologist among the Historians and Other Essays* (New York: Oxford University Press, 1984), 224–54. Also A. Appadurai, "Numbers in the Colonial Imagination," in C. A. Breckenridge and P. van der Veer (eds.), *Orientalism and the Postcolonial Predicament: Perspectives on South Asia* (Philadelphia: University of Pennsylvania Press, 1993), 314–40; Nicholas Dirks, *Castes of Mind. Colonialism and the Making of Modern India* (Princeton, NJ: Princeton University Press, 2001); Timothy Mitchell, *The Rule of Experts: Egypt, Technopolitics and Modernity* (Berkeley: University of California Press, 2002).

7. See, for example, Mitchell's discussion of the 1917 census in Eygpt: Mitchell, *The Rule of Experts*, 122.

8. Dirks, *Castes of Mind*.

9. J. Athelstane Baines, "The Population of the British Empire," *Journal of the Royal Statistical Society*, 69, 2 (1906), 441.

10. A.J. Christopher, "The Quest for a Census of the British Empire c. 1840–1940," *Journal of Historical Geography*, 34, 2 (2008), 268–85; Karl Ittmann, *A Problem of Great Importance: Population, Race and Power in the British Empire, 1918–1973* (Berkeley: University of California Press, 2014).

11. Higgs, *The Information State in England*, 79; Tom Crook and Glen O'Hara (eds.), *Statistics and the Public Sphere: Numbers and People in Modern Britain, c 1800–2000* (London: Routledge, 2011).

12. Matthew Edney, *Mapping an Empire: The Geographical Construction of British India 1765–1843* (Chicago: University of Chicago Press, 1997); Patrick Joyce, *The State of Freedom: A Social History of the British State since 1800* (Cambridge: Cambridge University Press, 2013), ch. 1; Mitchell, *The Rule of Experts*.

13. Brewer, *Sinews of Power*; Miles Ogborn, *Spaces of Modernity: London's Geographies, 1680–1780* (London: Guilford, 1998), ch. 5; Philip Harling, *The Modern British State: An Historical Introduction* (Cambridge: Polity, 2001); Patrick O'Brien, "The Political Economy of British Taxation, 1660–1815," *Economic History Review*, 41 (1988), 1–32.

14. William J Ashworth, *Customs and Excise: Trade, Production and Consumption in England, 1640–1845* (Oxford: Oxford University Press, 2003), 363.

15. Martin J. Daunton, *Trusting Leviathan: The Politics of Taxation in Britain, 1799–1914* (Cambridge: Cambridge University Press, 2001); idem., *Just Taxes: The Politics of Taxation in Britain, 1914–1979* (Cambridge: Cambridge University

Press, 2002). *Pace* Daunton, it was the anonymous and disinterested nature of the system, as much as its cheapness and efficiency, that allowed Britons to trust the state.

16. Ranajit Guha, *A Rule of Property for Bengal: An Essay on the Idea of Permanent Settlement* (Durham, NC: Duke University Press, 1996 [1963]); Shankar Madhave Pagar, *The Indian Income Tax: Its History, Theory and Practice* (Sayaji Gunj Baroda: Lakshmi Vilas Press, 1920); Ritu Birla, *Stages of Capital: Law, Culture and Market Governance in Late Colonia India* (Durham, NC: Duke University Press, 2009).

17. David Vincent, *The Culture of Secrecy Britain, 1832–1988* (Oxford: Oxford University Press, 1999); James Vernon, *Hunger. A Modern History* (Cambridge, MA: Harvard University Press, 2007); Higgs, *The Information State in England*.

18. Jon Agar, *The Government Machine: A Revolutionary History of the Computer* (Cambridge, MA: MIT Press, 2003).

19. Oliver MacDonagh, "Delegated Legislation and Administrative Decretions in the 1850s," *Victorian Studies*, 2, 1 (1958), 29–44; G. Kitson Clark, "'Statesmen in Disguise': Reflections on the History of the Civil Service," *Historical Journal*, 2, 1 (1959), 19–39; D.M. Young, *The Colonial Office in the Early Nineteenth Century* (1961); B. Cohn, "The Recruitment and Training of British Civil Servants in India," in *An Anthropologist among the Historians*, 500–553; Roy MacLeod (ed.), *Government and Expertise: Specialists, Administrators and Professionals, 1860–1919* (Cambridge: Cambridge University Press,1988).

20. H. Finer, *The British Civil Service* (London: Fabian Society, 1937).

21. Although it was also a product of a set of bureaucratic routines and practices. The filing system is a good example of this. Each issue was assigned its own file, and as it circulated through the department different individuals would provide their own interpretations of its contents in an act of collaborative deliberation that subordinated individual opinion to a disinterested survey of the history and issues at stake. Clark, "'Statesmen in Disguise'"; Oliver MacDonagh, *Early Victorian Government, 1830–1870* (London: Weidenfeld and Nicholson, 1977); Cohn, *An Anthropologist among the Historians*, 500–553; Patrick Joyce, "Filing the Raj: Political Technologies of the Imperial British State," in Tony Bennet and Patrick Joyce (eds.), *Material Powers: Cultural Studies, History and the Material Turn* (New York: Routledge, 2010), 102–23.

22. *The Civil Service, Vol. 3, Social Survey of the Civil Service: Evidence Submitted to the Committee under the Chairmanship of Lord Fulton, 1966–68* (London: H.M.S.O., 1969, ch. 1; Vincent, *The Culture of Secrecy*; Joyce, *The State of Freedom*, ch. 3.

23. Chris Otter, *The Victorian Eye. A Political History of Light and Vision in Britain, 1800–1910* (Chicago: University of Chicago Press, 2008), ch. 3; Tom Crook,

"Sanitary Inspection and the Public Sphere in Late Victorian and Edwardian Britain," *Social History*, 32, 4 (2007), 369–93.

24. Vincent, *The Culture of Secrecy*.

25. David Taylor, *The New Police in Nineteenth Century England* (Manchester: Manchester University Press, 1997); V.A.C. Gatrell, "Crime, Authority and the Police-Man State," in F.M.L. Thompson (ed.), *The Cambridge Social History of Britain 1750–1950, Vol.3* (Cambridge: Cambridge University Press, 1990), 243–310.

26. Headrick, *Tools of Empire*, 84.

27. Derek Gregory, "The Friction of Distance: Information Circulation and the Mails in Early Nineteenth Century England," *Journal of Historical Geography*, 13, 2 (1987), 130–54; M.J. Daunton, *Royal Mail: The Post Office since 1840* (London: Athlone, 1985).

28. F.C. Mather, "The Railways, the Electric Telegraphy and Public Order during the Chartist Period, 1837–48," *History*, 38, 132 (1953), 40–53; Headrick, *Tools of Empire*, ch. 11; idem., *Tentacles of Progress: Technology Transfer in the Age of Imperialism, 1850–1940* (New York: Oxford University Press, 1988), ch. 4.

29. Walter Bagehot, *The English Constitution* (Oxford: Oxford University Press, [1867] 2009). My thanks to Seth Koven for once again knowing my arguments better than me.

30. The architect for the new Palace of Westminster, Sir Charles Barry, also designed the new layout of Trafalgar Square with its fountains.

31. G. Alex Bremner, "Nation and Empire in the Government Architecture of Mid-Victorian London: The Foreign and India Office Reconsidered," *Historical Journal*, 48, 3 (2005), 703–42; George S. Dugdale, *Whitehall through the Centuries* (London: Phoenix House, 1950); Susan Foreman, *From Palace to Power: An Illustrated History of Whitehall* (Brighton: Alpha Press, 1995).

32. Thomas Metcalf, *An Imperial Vision: Victorian Architecture and Britain's Raj.* (Berkeley: University of California Press, 1989).

33. For an early and intriguing example see Barbara Metcalf, "On the Cusp of Colonial Modernity: Administration, Women and Islam in Princely Bhopal," presented at "Modernity, Diversity and the Public Sphere: Negotiating Religious Identities in 18th–20th Century India." Max-Weber-Kolleg, University of Erfurt, Germany, September 23–25, 2010.

34. Richard Price, *Making Empire: Colonial Encounters and the Creation of Imperial Rule in Nineteenth Century Africa* (Cambridge: Cambridge University Press, 2008), chs. 8 and 9.

35. Terry Ranger, "The Invention of Tradition in Colonial Africa," in Eric Hobsbawm and Terry Ranger (eds.), *The Invention of Tradition* (Cambridge:

Cambridge University Press, 1983); Mahmood Mamdani, *Citizen and Subject: Contemporary Africa and the Legacy of Late Colonialism* (Princeton, NJ: Princeton University Press, 1996); Thomas Metcalf, *Ideologies of the Raj* (Cambridge: Cambridge University Press, 1997); David Cannadine, *Ornamentalism: How the British Saw Their Empire* (London: Allen Lane, 2001).

36. Philip Mason, *The Men Who Ruled India, Vol. 2, The Guardians* (New York: St. Martins, 1954); Clive Dewey, *Anglo-Indian Attitudes: The Mind of the Indian Civil Service* (London: Hambledon, 1993); L. H. Gann and P. Duingnan, *The Rulers of British Africa, 1870–1914* (Stanford, CA: Stanford University Press, 1978); Anthony Kirk Greene, *Symbol of Authority: The British District Officer in Africa* (London: I.B. Tauris, 2006).

37. Nicola Sheldon, "The School Attendance Officer 1900–1939: From Policeman to Welfare Worker?" *History of Education*, 36, 6 (2007), 735–46, Seth Koven, *Slumming: Sexual and Social Politics in Victorian London* (Princeton, NJ: Princeton University Press, 2006); Harry Hendrick, *Child Welfare: England, 1872–1989* (London: Routledge, 1994).

4. ASSOCIATING WITH STRANGERS

1. T. B. Macaulay, *The History of England, Vol. 3* (London: Longmans, Green and Co., ([1848] 1898), ch. 3; Jürgen Habermas, *The Structural Transformation of the Public Sphere* (Cambridge: Polity, 1989).

2. James Vernon, *Politics and the People: A Study in English Political Culture and Communication, 1815–1867* (Cambridge: Cambridge University Press, 1993); Jon Lawrence, "Paternalism, Class, and the British Path of Modernity," in Simon Gunn and James Vernon (eds.), *The Peculiarities of Liberal Modernity in Imperial Britain* (Berkeley: University of California Press, 2011); Patrick Joyce, *The Rule of Freedom: Liberalism and the Modern City* (London: Verso, 2003).

3. Peter Clark, *British Clubs and Societies 1580–1800: The Origins of an Associational World* (Oxford: Clarendon Press, 2000), 90 and 128.

4. Jessica Harland, *Builders of Empire: Freemasons and British Imperialism, 1717–1927* (Chapel Hill: University of North Carolina Press, 2007), 2–4.

5. Alastair J. Reid, *United We Stand: A History of Britain's Trade Unions* (London: Penguin Books, 2005).

6. Clark, *British Clubs and Societies 1580–1800*, 70.

7. Penelope Ismay, *Trust among Strangers: Securing British Modernity "by Way of Friendly Society," 1780s—1870s* (Berkeley: University of California Press, 2010).

8. This paragraph draws entirely upon Reid, *United We Stand*.

9. Cricket was the precocious exception, with the rules of the game having been codified in the eighteenth century and administered by the Marylebone Cricket Club (better known as the MCC) since 1787. Tellingly, the parish remained the level of team organization until a nationally organized county structure was created in 1890.

10. John Brewer, *Party Ideology and Popular Politics at the Accession of George III* (Cambridge: Cambridge University Press, 1976), 175.

11. The exception was the loyalist Association for the Preservation of Liberty and Property that reputedly boasted 2,000 branches and a strong central organizing committee in London. In contrast, there were just 120 Political Unions clustered mainly in the north and midlands, boasting a membership of 18,000 and attracting more than 200,000 to all their meetings. Nancy LoPatin, *Political Unions, Popular Politics, and the Great Reform Act of 1832* (Basingstoke: Palgrave Macmillan, 1999); Robert Dozier, *For King, Constitution and Country: The English Loyalists and the French Revolution* (Lexington: University Press of Kentucky, 1983).

12. James Epstein, *The Lion of Freedom: Feargus O'Connor and the Chartist Movement, 1832–1842* (Brighton: Croom Helm, 1982); John Belchem and James Epstein, "The Gentleman Leader Revisited," *Social History,* 22, 2 (1997), 174–93.

13. Dorothy Thompson, *The Chartists: Popular Politics in the Industrial Revolution* (London: Pantheon, 1984), 49; Aled Jones, "Chartist Journalism and Print Culture in Britain, 1830–1855," in J. Allen and O. Ashton (eds.), *Papers for the People: A Study of the Chartist Press* (London: Merlin Press), 3–24.

14. Malcolm Chase, "National Charter Association of Great Britain (*act.* 1840–1858)," *Oxford Dictionary of National Biography.* www.oxforddnb.com/view/theme/92506

15. Paul Pickering and Alex Tyrell, *The People's Bread: A History of the Anti-Corn Law League* (London: Leicester University Press, 2000).

16. Jon Lawrence, *Electing Our Masters: The Hustings in British Politics from Hogarth to Blair* (Oxford: Oxford University Press, 2009), 78–80. James Thompson, "'Pictorial Lies?' Posters and Politics in Britain, c. 1880–1914," *Past and Present,* 197 (2007), 177–200; Kathryn Rix, "The Party Agent and English Electoral Culture, 1880–1906." PhD diss. University of Cambridge, 2001.

17. Derek Beales, "Parliamentary Parties and the Independent Member, 1800–1860," in Robert Robson (ed.), *Ideas and Institutions in Victorian Britain* (London: Bell, 1967), 1–19.

18. Similarly, both political parties sought to harness the industry and support of women: the Conservatives with the Primrose League (1883) and the

Liberals through the Women's Liberal Federation (1886). The latter's membership peaked at 133,125 by 1912, still nowhere near the size of its competitor, which boasted 650,000 members for that same year. Anthony Seldon and Peter Snowdon, *The Conservative Party* (Stroud: Sutton, 2004), 211.

19. Moisey Ostrogorski, *Democracy and the Organization of Political Parties*. 2 vols. (London: Macmillan, 1902).

20. John Vincent, *The Formation of the British Liberal Party 1857–1868* (London: Constable, 1966); Patrick Joyce, *Visions of the People: Industrial England the Question of Class, c. 1848–1914* (Cambridge: Cambridge University Press, 1991); Eugenio Biagini, *Liberty, Retrenchment and Reform: Popular Liberalism in the Age of Gladstone, 1860–1880* (Cambridge: Cambridge University Press, 1992).

21. Jon Lawrence, *Speaking for the People: Party, Language and Popular Politics in England 1867–1914* (Cambridge: Cambridge University Press, 1998); idem., "Labour: The Myths It Has Lived By," in D. Tanner, P. Thane, N. Tiratsoo (eds.), *Labour's First Century* (Cambridge: Cambridge University Press, 2007), 341–66.

22. Laura Mayhall, *The Militant Suffrage Movement: Citizenship and Resistance in Britain, 1860–1930* (Oxford: Oxford University Press, 2003).

23. Benedict Anderson, *Imagined Communities; Reflections on the Origins and Spread of Nationalism* (London: Verso, 1983).

24. Peter Lake and Steve Pincus, "Rethinking the Public Sphere in Early Modern England," *Journal of British Studies*, 45, 2 (2006), 270–92.

25. Thomas de Quincey, "The English Mail-Coach," *Blackwood's Edinburgh Magazine* (October,1849)..

26. A.P. Wadsworth, "Newspaper Circulations, 1800–1954," *Proceedings of the Manchester Statistical Society* (1955); Aled Jones, *Powers of the Press: Newspapers, Power and the Public in Nineteenth-Century England* (Aldershot: Scolar, 1996).

27. Jeremy Black, "The Development of the Provincial Newspaper Press in the Eighteenth Century," *Journal for Eighteenth Century Studies*, 14, 2 (2008), 159–70; Andrew Walker, "The Development of the Provincial Press in England c. 1780–1914," *Journalism Studies*, 7, 3 (2006), 373–86; Wadsworth, "Newspaper Circulations 1800–1954."

28. Donald Read, *The Power of News: The History of Reuters 1849–1989* (Oxford: Oxford University Press, 1992).

29. Simon Potter, *News and the British World: The Emergence of an Imperial Press System* (Oxford: Clarendon Press, 2003); Chandrika Kaul, *Reporting the Raj: The British Press and India, c. 1880–1922* (Manchester: Manchester University Press, 2003); idem (ed.), *Media and the British Empire* (Basingstoke: Palgrave Macmillan, 2006). There were also English-language papers across the infor-

mal empire in places like Argentina and Brazil. *The Newspaper Press Directory and Advertisers Guide* (London: Mitchell, 1905).

30. Andrew Walker, *A Skyful of Freedom: Sixty Years of the BBC World Service* (London: Broadside Books, 1992); Caroline Ritter, "The Cultural Project of the Late British Empire" (Ph.D diss. University of California-Berkeley, 2015, forthcoming).

31. James Thompson, *British Political Culture and the Idea of "Public Opinion," 1867–1914* (Cambridge: Cambridge University Press, 2013). Thomas Osborne and Nikolas Rose, "Do the Social Sciences Create Phenomena: The Case of Public Opinion Research," *British Journal of Sociology,* 50, 3 (1999), 367–96; Brian Harrison, *The Transformation of British Politics 1860–1995* (Oxford: Oxford University Press, 1996), 230–43.

32. Derek Hirst, *The Representatives of the People? Voters and Voting in England under the Early Stuarts* (Cambridge: Cambridge University Press, 1975); Mark Kishlansky, *Parliamentary Selection: Social and Political Choice in Early Modern England* (Cambridge: Cambridge University Press, 1986); J. H. Plumb, "The Growth of the Electorate in England from 1600–1715," *Past and Present,* 45 (1969), 90–116.

33. Lewis Namier, *The Structure of Politics at the Accession of George III* (London: Macmillan, 1929); Frank O'Gorman, *Voters, Patrons, and Parties: The Unreformed Electoral System of Hanoverian England 1734–1832* (Oxford: Oxford University Press, 1989). There were twelve elections between 1689 and 1715 until the Septennial Act (1715) helped ensure that were only thirteen more for the rest of the century. There was a last flurry of nine held between 1802 and 1831.

34. For variations on types of constituencies see O'Gorman, *Voters, Parties and Patrons;* John Phillips, *Electoral Behaviour in Unreformed England* (Princeton, NJ: Princeton University Press, 1982); R. G. Thorne, *The House of Commons, 1754–1790.* 2 vols. (London: Secker and Warburg, 1986).

35. In the rural counties the franchise was nominally extended to include £10 copy-holders and leaseholders as well as £50 tenants, but this merely standardized the broad definition unevenly applied to the 40-shilling freehold qualification under the unreformed system.

36. Katherine Rix, "'The Elimination of Corrupt Practices in British Election'? Reassessing the Impact of the 1883 Corrupt Practices Act," *English Historical Review,* 123 (2008), 65–97; K. Theodore Hoppen, "Roads to Democracy: Electioneering and Corruption in Nineteenth Century England and Ireland," *History,* 91 (1996), 553–71; Alan Heesom, "'Legitimate' versus 'Illegitimate' Influences": Aristocratic Electioneering in Mid-Victorian Britain," *Parliamentary History,* 7, 2 (1988), 282–305; C. Seymour, *The Elimination of Corrupt Practices in British Elections, 1868–1911* (New Haven: Yale University Press, 1915).

37. Campaigns for the secret ballot began in 1835, long before the creation of the Ballot Society (1853), and were small and insignificant. These were confined to annual motions in Parliament by idiosyncratic MPs, and the occasional burst of petitioning (which culminated in 1868–69 with ninety-nine petitions and a total of seven thousand signatures). Frank O'Gorman, "The Secret Ballot in Nineteenth Century Britain," in R. Bertrand, J.-L. Briquet and P. Pels (eds.), *Cultures of Voting: The Hidden History of the Secret Ballot* (London: C. Hurst and Co., 2007); Malcolm and Tom Crook, "The Advent of the Secret Ballot in Britain and France, 1789–1914: From Public Assembly to Private Compartment," *History*, 92, 308 (2007), 449–71; idem., "Reforming Voting Practices in a Global Age: The Making and Remaking of the Modern Secret Ballot in Britain, France and the United States, c. 1600–c. 1950," *Past and Present*, 212 (August 2011), 199–237; Elaine Hadley, *Living Liberalism: Practical Citizenship in Mid-Victorian Britain* (Chicago: University of Chicago Press, 2010), ch. 4.

38. O'Gorman, "The Secret Ballot in Nineteenth Century Britain," 33.

39. Matthew Roberts, "Resisting 'Arithmocracy': Parliament, Community, and the Third Reform Act," *Journal of British Studies*, 50, 2 (2011), 381–409. For two pertinent intellectual histories see Sandra Den Otter, "'Thinking in Communities': Late Nineteenth-Century Liberals, Idealists and the Retrieval of Community," *Parliamentary History*, 16 (1997), 67–84; Karuna Mantena, *Alibis of Empire: Henry Maine and the Ends of Liberal Imperialism* (Princeton, NJ: Princeton University Press, 2009).

40. It was, however, cunningly renamed "dual" voting to distinguish it from the practice, first introduced in 1818 but finally abolished in 1918, of electors being able to vote multiple times in a number of constituencies if their property or other qualifications allowed them to do so. This reduced the number of plural voters of all kinds from more than 500,000 before the war to 159,000 under the business franchise and 68,000 under the university franchise.

41. Nicoletta Gullace, *The Blood of Our Sons: Men, Women and the Renegotiation of British Citizenship during the Great War* (Basingstoke: Palgrave Macmillan, 2004), 167–94; Joseph Meisel, "A Magnificent Fungus on the Political Tree: The Growth of University Representation in the United Kingdom, 1832–1950," *History of Universities*, 23, 1 (2008), 109–86. 1948 saw the final abolition of the last remaining ten double-member constituencies.

42. Mrinalini Sinha, *Spectres of Mother India: The Global Restructuring of an Empire* (Durham, NC: Duke University Press, 2006), ch. 5; Mahmood Mamdani, *Citizen and Subject: Contemporary Africa and the Legacy of Late Colonialism* (Princeton, NJ: Princeton University Press, 1996).

43. David Gilmartin, "Election Law and the 'People' in Colonial and Post-colonial India," in D. Chakrabarty, R. Majumdar, and A. Sartori (eds.), *From the Colonial to the Postcolonial: India and Pakistan in Transition* (Delhi: Oxford University Press, 2007), 55–82; Christophe Jaffrelot, "Voting in India: Electoral Symbols, the Party System and the Collective Citizen," and Peter Pels, "Imagining Elections: Modernity, Mediation, and the Secret Ballot in Late Colonial Tanganayika," in Bertrand et al. (eds.), *Cultures of Voting*.

44. An argument made of the French republican model of democracy by Pierre Rosanvallon, *Democracy: Past, Present and Future* (New York: Columbia University Press, 2007); *Counter Democracy: Politics in an Age of Mistrust* (Cambridge: Cambridge University Press 2008).

5. AN ECONOMY OF STRANGERS

1. Eric Hobsbawm, *Industry and Empire: The Making of Modern English Society, 1750 to the Present Day* (London: Pantheon, 1968), xi.

2. Peter Mathias, *The First Industrial Nation: The Economic History of Britain 1700–1914* (London: Methuen, 1969); Gareth Stedman Jones, *An End of Poverty? A Historical Debate* (New York: Columbia University Press, 2004), ch. 4; D.C. Coleman, *Myth, History and the Industrial Revolution* (London: Hambledon, 1992), ch. 1.

3. Although during the past thirty years scholars have taken the revolution out of industrialization, there is a marked revival of interest in Britain's Industrial Revolution as a transformative world event. M. Berg and P. Hudson, "Rehabilitating the Industrial Revolution," *Economic History Review*, 45, 1 (1992): 24–50; Jan de Vries, *The Industrious Revolution: Consumer Behaviour and the Household Economy 1650 to the Present* (Cambridge: Cambridge University Press, 2008); Robert Allen, *The British Industrial Revolution in Global Perspective* (Cambridge: Cambridge University Press, 2009); Joel Mokyr, *The Enlightened Economy: An Economic History of Britain 1700–1850* (New Haven: Yale University Press, 2010); E. A. Wrigley, *Energy and the Industrial Revolution* (Cambridge: Cambridge University Press, 2010).

4. Harold Perkin, *The Origins of Modern English Society, 1780–1880* (London: Routledge, Kegan and Paul, 1969); Allan MacFarlane, *The Culture of Capitalism* (Oxford: Blackwell, 1987); de Vries, *The Industrious Revolution*.

5. Avner Grief, "The Birth of Impersonal Exchange: The Community Responsibility System and Impartial Justice," *Journal of Economic Perspectives*, 20, 2 (2006), 221–36. For more nuanced accounts see Olivia Constable, *Housing the Stranger in the Mediterranean World: Lodging, Trade, and Travel in Late Antiquity*

and the Middle Ages (Cambridge: Cambridge University Press, 2003); Francesca Trivellato, *The Familiarity of Strangers: The Sephardic Diaspora, Livorno, and Cross Cultural Trade in the Early Modern Period* (New Haven: Yale University Press, 2009). See also Philip D. Curtin, *Cross-Cultural Trade in World History* (Cambridge: Cambridge University Press, 1984).

6. C. Knick Harley, "Trade: Discovery, Mercantilism and Technology," in Roderick Floud and Paul Johnson (eds.), *The Cambridge Economic History of Britain, Vol. 1, Industrialisation 1700–1860* (Cambridge: Cambridge University Press, 2004), 175–203; Ronald Findlay and Kevin O'Rourke, *Power and Plenty: Trade, War and the World Economy in the Second Millennium* (Princeton, NJ: Princeton University Press, 2007), chs. 4 and 5; Kevin O'Rourke and Jeffrey Williamson, "After Columbus: Explaining Global Trade Boom 1500–1800," *Journal of Economic History*, 60, 2 (2002): 417–56.

7. E.P. Thompson, "The Moral Economy of the English Crowd in the Eighteenth Century," *Past and Present*, 50, 1 (1971), 76–136.

8. John J. McCusker, "The Demise of Distance: The Business Press and the Origins of the Information Revolution in the Early Modern Atlantic World," *American Historical Review*, 110, 2 (2005), 295–321; Natasha Glaisyer, *The Culture of Commerce in England 1660–1720* (Woodbridge: Boydell Press, 2006), ch. 1; David Hancock, *Citizens of the World: London Merchants and the Integration of the British Atlantic Community, 1735–1785* (Cambridge: Cambridge University Press, 1995); R. Grassby, *The Business Community of Seventeenth Century England* (Cambridge: Cambridge University Press, 1995); Pat Hudson, "Industrial Organisation and Structure," in Floud and Johnson (eds.), *The Cambridge Economic History of Britain, Vol. 1*, 28–56.

9. Ranald C. Michie, *The London Stock Exchange: A History* (Oxford: Oxford University Press, 1999), 15.

10. Anne Murphy, *The Origins of English Financial Markets: Investment and Speculation Before the South Sea Bubble* (Cambridge: Cambridge University Press, 2012), chs. 4 and 5; Alex Preda, *Framing Finance: The Boundaries of Markets and Modern Capitalism* (Chicago: Chicago University Press, 2009), 113.

11. Other elements of the City's financial services underwent similar transformations. Merchant banks, whose liquidity often rested on the reputation of their families (Barings, Warburgs, Rothschilds), established the London Clearing House in 1773 to facilitate transactions among its thirty-one members. The following year those involved in marine insurance moved Lloyds from its coffee house to the Royal Exchange and established a governing committee that set the terms of admission.

12. Mokyr, *The Enlightened Economy,* 28–29.

13. Quoted in James Taylor, *Creating Capitalism: Joint Stock Enterprise in British Politics and Culture, 1800–1870* (Woodbridge: Boydell Press, 2006), 27.

14. Taylor, *Creating Capitalism;* Mark Freeman, Robin Pearson, and James Taylor, *Shareholder Democracies? Corporate Governance in Britain and Ireland before 1850* (Chicago: University of Chicago Press, 2012).

15. Charles Babbage, *On the Economy of Machinery and Manufacturers* (London: Charles Knight, 1832); A. Ure, *Philosophy of Manufacturers* (London: Charles Knight, 1835).

16. David Cannadine, *The Rise and Fall of Class in Britain* (New Haven: Yale University Press, 2000), 117–18.

17. Mokyr, *The Enlightened Economy,* 3.

18. Wayne Parsons, *The Power of the Financial Press: Journalism and Economic Opinion in Britain and America* (New Brunswick, NJ: Rutgers University Press, 1989), 12; John J. McCusker, "The Business Press in England before 1775," in his *Essays in the Economic History of the Atlantic World* (London, 1997); idem., "The Demise of Distance"; L. Neal, "The Rise of a Financial Press: London and Amsterdam, 1681–1810," *Business History,* 30 (1988), 163–78; Murphy, *The Origins of English Financial Markets,* chs. 4 and 5; Julian Hoppit, "The Contexts and Contours of British Economic Literature 1660–1760," *Historical Journal,* 49, 1 (2006), 79–110.

19. "The Merchant who wanted to know what was the prices of indigoes at India House; what ships were sailing for Jamaica ... what firms had gone under in a commercial crisis ... had to obtain his news by the exchange of information with his fellows. From an hour's talk in mixed company he could learn more than from the Gazettes of a week." Quoted in Parsons, *The Power of the Financial Press,* 13.

20. Parsons, *The Power of the Financial Press,* 17; J.J. McCusker and C. Gravesteijn, *The Beginnings of Commercial and Financial Journalism* (Amsterdam: Nederlandsch Economisch-Historisch Archief, 1991), 288–89.

21. Natasha Glaisyer, "Calculating Credibility: Print Culture, Trust and Economic Figures in Early Eighteenth-Century England," *Economic History Review,* 60, 4 (2007), 685–711; idem, *The Culture of Commerce in England 1660–1720,* ch. 1.

22. Desmond FitzGibbon, "Assembling the Property Market in Imperial Britain, c. 1750–1925." PhD diss. University of California-Berkeley, 2011, 19.

23. Parsons, *The Power of the Financial Press;* Mary Poovey, *The Financial System in Nineteenth-Century Britain* (New York: Oxford University Press, 2002), 25–32.

24. The *Financial Times* described itself as the "friend of the honest financier, the bona fide investor, the respectable Broker, the genuine director, the legitimate speculator." Parsons, *The Power of the Financial Press*, 38–39. Preda claims that no less than fifty-two periodicals (many short lived) related to the stock exchange were published during the nineteenth century. Preda, *Framing Finance*, 89.

25. Charles Duguid, *How to Read the Money Article* (London, 1901). In 1936 it was still selling in its sixth edition.

26. *Beeton's Guide Book to the Stock Exchange and Money Markets: With Hints to Investors, and the Chances of Speculators* (London: Ward, Lock and Tyler, 1870); *Beeton's Guide to Investing Money with Safety and Profit* (London: Ward, Lock and Tyler, 1872); Charles Castelli, *The Rationale of Market Fluctuations* (London: F.C. Mathieson, 1876); idem., *The Theory of "Options" in Stocks and Shares* (London: F.C. Mathieson, 1877); ; A.J. Wilson, *Practical Hints to Investors and Some Words to Speculators* (London: C. Wilson, 1897); C.H. Thorpe, *How to Invest and How to Speculate : Explanatory of the Details of Stock Exchange Business, and the Main Classes of Securities Dealt In; Together with a Glossary of Terms in Common Use* (London: G. Richards, 1901); Ernest Wallis, *Hints to Small Investors: A Practical Handbook for Their Use* (London: The Money Maker, 1901).

27. Leading editors like Walter Bagehot and Charles Duguid (city editor for the *Morning Post*) also published books explaining the stock market's development as an institution. Walter Bagehot, *Lombard Street: A Description of the Money Market* (London, 1873); Charles Duguid, *The Story of the Stock Exchange: Its History and Position* (London, 1901).

28. Michael O'Leary, Wanda J. Orlikowski, and JoAnne Yates, "Distributed Work over the Centuries: Trust and Control in the Hudson's Bay Company, 1670–1826," in Pamela J. Hinds and Sara Kiesler (eds.), *Distributed Work* (Cambridge, MA: MIT Press, 2002), 27–54; Ann M. Carlos and Santhi Hejeebus, "Specific Information and the English Chartered Companies, 1650–1750," in Leos Muller and Jari Ojala (eds.), *Information Flows: New Approaches in the Historical Study of Business Information* (Helsinki: Finnish Literature Society, 2007), 139–68; David Hancock, *Citizens of the World*, ch. 3; Miles Ogborn, *Indian Ink: Script and Print in the Making of the English East India Company* (Chicago: University of Chicago Press, 2007), ch. 3.

29. Caitlin Rosenthal, *From Slavery to Scientific Management: Accounting for Control in Antebellum America* (Cambridge, MA: Harvard University Press, forthcoming).

30. Ewing Matheson's *The Depreciation of Factories, Mines and Industrial Undertakings and their Valuation,* published in 1884, had run to a fourth edition

by 1910; Emile Garcke's *Factory Accounts in Principle and Practice,* first published in 1887, went to seven editions by 1922; and George Norton's *Textile Manufacturer's Book-Keeping for the Counting House, Mill and Warehouse,* first published in 1889, was in its fifth edition by 1931. See also Thomas Millar, *Management Book-Keeping for the Manufacturer, Wholesaler and Retailer* (London: Charles and Edwin Layton, 1910); Edward T. Elbourne, *Factory Administration and Accounts: A Book of Reference with Tables and Specimen Forms for Managers, Engineers and Accountants* (London: Longmans, Green and Co., 1914). Sidney Pollard, *The Genesis of Modern Management: A Study of the Industrial Revolution in Great Britain* (Cambridge, MA: Harvard University Press, 1965), 248.

31. JoAnne Yates, *Control through Communication: The Rise of System in American Management* (Baltimore: Johns Hopkins University Press, 1989).

32. Benedict Anderson, *Imagined Communities: Reflections on the Origin and Spread of Nationalism* (London: Verso, 1983); Linda Colley, *Britons: The Forging of a Nation, 1707–1837* (New Haven: Yale University Press, 1992); Manu Goswami, *Producing India: From Colonial Economy to National Space* (Chicago: University of Chicago Press, 2004).

33. Deborah Valenze, *The Social Life of Money in the English Past* (Cambridge: Cambridge University Press, 2006).

34. Craig Muldrew, *The Economy of Obligation: The Culture of Credit and Social Relations in Early Modern England* (Basingstoke: Palgrave Macmillan, 1998).

35. Carl Wennerlind, *Casualties of Credit: The English Financial Revolution* (Cambridge, MA: Harvard University Press, 2011); Glaisyer, "Calculating Credibility."

36. Sir Albert Feaveryear, *The Pound Sterling: A History of English Money,* 2nd ed. (Oxford: Clarendon Press, 1963), 136–40.

37. Sir John Clapham, *The Bank of England: A History, Vol. 1* (Cambridge: Cambridge University Press, 1944), ch. 1.

38. Randall McGowen, "From Pillory to Gallows: The Punishment of Forgery in the Age of the Financial Revolution," *Past and Present,* 165, 1 (1999), 107–40.

39. Randall McGowen, "The Bank of England and the Policing of Forgery, 1797–1821," *Past and Present,* (2005), 81–116.

40. In fact, the gold standard was only fully established by the 1844 Bank Act as before that a fifth of bank reserves were allowed to be held in silver. Ted Wilson, *Battles for the Standard: Bimetallism and the Spread of the Gold Standard in the Nineteenth Century* (Aldershot: Ashgate, 2000), ch. 2.

41. As late as the 1890s a Bimetallic League was founded in Manchester arguing that currency reform was essential to revive Lancashire's textile

exports. Its arguments were strong enough to merit riposte by the Gold Standard Defence Association. Ewen Green, "Rentiers versus Producers? The Political Economy of the Bimetallic Controversy c. 1880–1898," *English Historical Review*, 103, (1988), 588–612; A.C. Howe, "Bimettalism, c. 1880–1898: A Controversy Re-Opened?" *English Historical Review* (1990), 377–91.

42. Timothy L. Alborn, "Coin and Country: Visions of Civilisation in the British Recoinage Debate, 1867–1891," *Journal of Victorian Culture*, 3, 2, (1998), 254.

43. Om Prakash, "On Coinage in Mugahl India," *Indian Economic and Social History Review*, 25, 4 (1988); Manu Goswmani, *Producing India: From Colonial Economy to National Space* (Chicago: Chicago University Press, 2004), 85–102; Amiya Kumar Bagchi, "Transition from Indian to British Indian Systems of Money and Banking 1800–1850," *Modern Asian Studies*, 19, 3 (1985), 501–19 (503); S. Ambirajan, *Political Economy and Monetary Management: India, 1766–1914* (Madras: Affiliated East-West Press, 1984).

44. However, as the gold standard made all currencies convertible to sterling, it was the persistence of tariffs that proved the greater impediment to trade. Barry Eichengreen, *Golden Fetters: The Gold Standard and the Great Depression, 1919–1939* (Oxford: Oxford University Press, 1996); Catherine Schenk, *The Decline of Sterling: Managing the Retreat of an International Currency, 1945–1992* (Cambridge: Cambridge University Press, 2010).

45. John J. McCusker, "Weights and Measures in the Colonial Sugar Trade: The Gallon and the Pound and their International Equivalents," in his *Essays in the Economic History of the Atlantic World* (London: Routledge, 1997), 84.

46. Ronald Zupko, *The Revolution in Measurement: Western European Weights and Measures since the Age of Science* (Philadelphia: American Philosophical Society, vol. 186, 1996), 25–26. Other elastic standards included the barrel, boll, bushel, cartload, hogshead, pipe, pot, and wagonload. See also R.D. Connor, *The Weights and Measures of England* (London: H.M.S.O, 1987); Daniel Headrick, *When Information Came of Age: Technologies of Knowledge in the Age of Reason and Revolution, 1700–1850* (New York: Oxford University Press, 2000), ch. 2.

47. McCusker, "Weights and Measures in the Colonial Sugar Trade," 85–87.

48. Zupko, *The Revolution in Measurement*, 178.

49. Goswami, *Producing India*, 86; Zupko, *The Revolution in Measurement*, 232–68.

50. There were fifteen estimates of national income made between 1667 and 1812. Julian Hoppit, "Political Arithmetic in Eighteenth Century Eng-

land," *Economic History Review*, 49, 3 (1996), 516–40; William Petty, *Political Arithmetic* (1690); idem, *Verbum Sapienti* (1691); William Playfair, *The Commercial and Political Atlas: Representing, by Means of Stained Copper-Plate Charts, the Progress of the Commerce, Revenues, Expenditure and Debts of England during the Whole of the Eighteenth Century* (Cambridge: Cambridge University Press, [1786] 2005).

51. Adam Tooze, *Statistics and the German State, 1900–1945: The Making of Modern Economic Knowledge* (Cambridge: Cambridge University Press, 2001). Goswami, *Producing India*, chs. 2 and 7. In Britain the state often lagged behind: although *The Economist* published its price indices in 1869, the Board of Trade did not follow suit until 1903.

52. Tooze, *Statistics and the German State, 1900–1945*, 9; idem, "Trouble with Numbers: Statistics, Politics, and History in the Construction of Weimar's Trade Balance, 1918–1924," *American Historical Review*, 113, 3 (2008), 678.

53. Timothy Mitchell, *The Rule of Experts: Egypt, Techno-Politics, Modernity* (Berkeley: University of California Press, 2002), 6. See also Jed Esty, *A Shrinking Island: Modernism and National Culture in England* (Princeton, NJ: Princeton University Press 2003), ch. 4.

54. On the continued inadequacies and haphazard nature of British economic statistics between the wars see C.F.Carter and A.D. Roy, *British Economic Statistics: A Report* (Cambridge: Cambridge University Press, 1954).

55. Jim Tomlinson, "Inventing 'Decline': The Falling Behind of the British Economy in the Postwar Years," *Economic History Review*, 49, 4 (1996), 731–57; idem, "Managing the Economy, Managing the People: Britain c. 1931–1970," *Economic History Review*, 58, 3 (2005), 555–85.

56. Walter Bagehot, "The Postulates of English Political Economy, No.1," *Fortnightly Review* (February 1876), 215; Julian Hoppitt, "The Contexts and Contours of British Economic Literature, 1660–1760," *Historical Journal*, 49, 1 (2006), 79–110; Catherine Gallagher, *The Body Economic: Life, Death and Sensation in Political Economy and the Victorian Novel* (Princeton, NJ: Princeton University Press, 2008).

57. Marion Fourcade, *Economists and Societies: Discipline and Profession in the United States, Britain and France, 1890s-1990s* (Princeton, NJ: Princeton University Press, 2009), ch. 3.

58. These paragraphs draw entirely from Michie, *The London Stock Exchange*.

59. W.A. Thomas, *The Provincial Stock Exchanges* (London: Cass, 1973).

60. Mokyr, *The Enlightened Economy*, 28–29.

61. Margo Finn, *The Character of Credit: Personal Debt in English Culture, 1740–1914* (Cambridge: Cambridge University Press, 2003), ch. 7.

62. This is central to Robert Roberts's account of his parents shop in Salford before the Great War. *The Classic Slum* (Manchester: Manchester University Press, 1971), ch. 5.

63. Josh Lauer, "From Rumor to Written Record: Credit Reporting and the Invention of Financial Identity in Nineteenth-Century America," *Technology and Culture,* 49, 2 (April 2008); "The Good Consumer: Credit Reporting and the Invention of Financial Identity in the United States, 1840–1940," *Enterprise and Society,* 11, 4 (2010), 686–94. I am greatly indebted to David Vincent for sharing with me his research notes on American credit agencies.

64. For one of many accounts John Fielden, *The Curse of the Factory System* (London: A. M. Kelley, [1836] 1969). Robert Gray, *The Factory Question and Industrial England, 1830–1860* (Cambridge: Cambridge University Press, 1996).

65. Patrick Joyce, *Work, Society and Politics: The Culture of the Factory in Late Victorian England* (Brighton: Methuen, 1981); Martin Weiner, *English Culture and the Decline of the Industrial Spirit, 1850–1980* (Cambridge: Cambridge University Press, 1981).

INDEX